1920

The 19th Amendment
gives women in the
United States the
right to vote.

SEXUAL
POLITICS

I dislike the "essentialist/ deconstructivist" dichoto- my. Most good work has elements of each, and we were well aware in 1970 that women's identity was socially constructed.

I don't think we looked at the social construction of "woman" as much as we looked at our experience.
—Sheila Levrant de Bretteville

The body is fixed in its physicality, and gender is socially constructed. Both of these things are true.
—Arlene Raven

Using sex organs to mythologize female experience is totally off the wall and pointless. . . . I would feel the same about a table covered with penises—turned off.
—Vivian Gornick

—Lucy Lippard

The cunt was the signifier for our myriad presence.
—Miriam Schapiro

Feminists were saying, Do work about yourself, about your own identity, whatever you want, do it. It was the feminists who consistently gave permission for this kind of art making.
—Tom Knechtel

The point was to try to make images of that which is not represented and to claim it too, to name it and claim it in a new way. You can see how that, then, would after a while be- come a celebration.
—Faith Wilding

And the art strategies of the eighties—autobiography, political activism, the transformation of self through multiple personae, the appropriation and cri- tique of mainstream culture—were these not the strategies forged by the same feminist art movement now so reviled by the art avant-garde?
—Terry Wolverton

If we are seeking validation from a male-oriented system, we will receive it in the coinage of that system and not on our own terms.
—Arlene Raven

How many artists truly politicize dif- ference by interro- gating their choices?
—bell hooks

SEXUAL POLITICS

Judy Chicago's *Dinner Party* in Feminist Art History

Amelia Jones

Editor

With essays by

Laura Cottingham

Amelia Jones

Susan Kandel

Anette Kubitza

Laura Meyer

Nancy Ring

UCLA at the **Armand Hammer Museum of Art and Cultural Center**

in association with

University of California Press

Berkeley   Los Angeles   London

Published with the assistance of the Getty Grant Program

Artists in the
Exhibition

"There's lots of

vagina in our work, but it is not about vaginas. Rather, we are inventing a new form language radiating a female power which cannot be conveyed in any other way at this time. . . . These images are universal, for they are about being a human body in the world . . . a holy body: which knows, thinks, pains, remembers, works, imagines, dreams, yearns, aspires, and which may not be violated. As women artists we are presenting an image of woman's body and spirit as that which cannot and must not be colonized either sexually, economically, or politically."

—Faith Wilding

FIG. 1
Faith Wilding. *Womb*, 1971 (cat. no. 6).

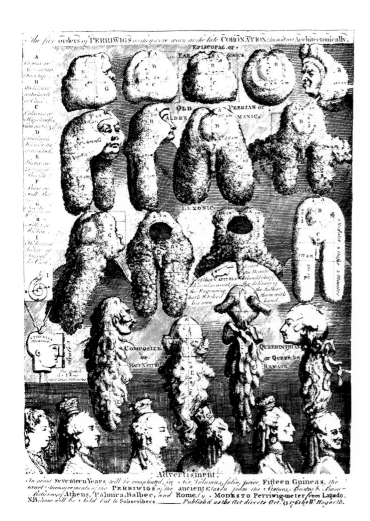

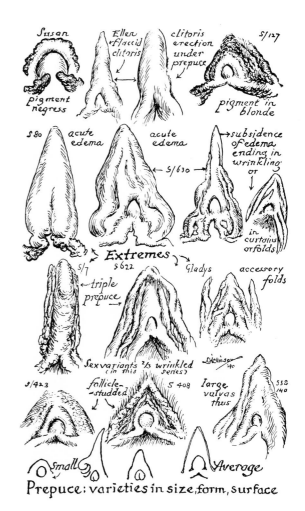

FIGS. 3–4
Mira Schor. *"Cunt,"* 1993; *"Penis,"* 1993 (cat. nos. 20–21).

FIG. 6
Hannah Wilke. *Seven Untitled Vaginal-Phallic and Excremental Sculptures,* 1960–63 (cat. no. 3).

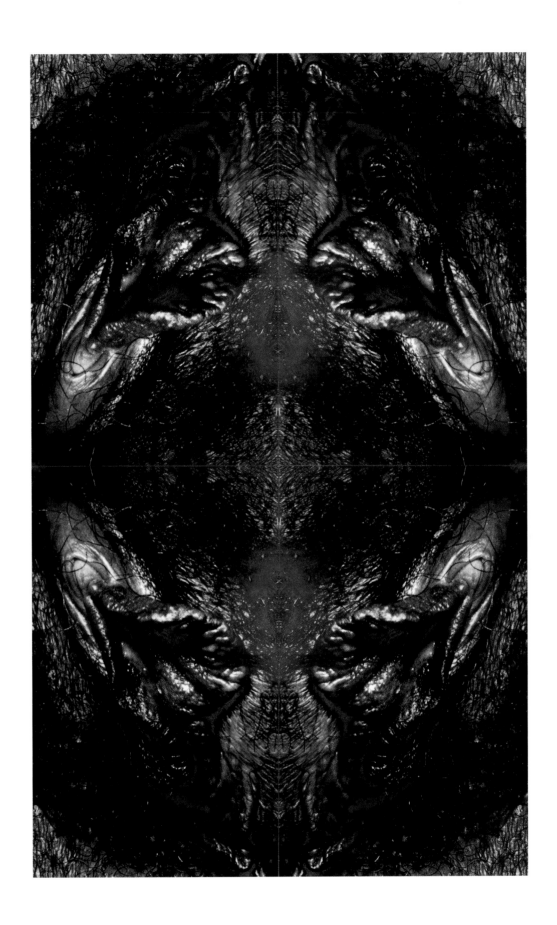

FIG. 7
Tee A. Corinne. *#40*, from the Yantras of Womanlove series, 1982 (cat. no. 14).

Sexual Politics:
Feminist Strategies,
Feminist Conflicts,
Feminist Histories

Amelia Jones

The first part of the title of this exhibition, *Sexual Politics*, alludes to Kate Millett's best-selling book of 1970, in which she theorizes "sex" (or "sexual difference," as we would say today) as a site of oppression and so a locus for political intervention. My reference to this book—with its polemical call for a politics oriented around "our system of sexual relationship . . . [as one] of dominance and subordinance"[1]—marks both my commitment to rethinking the terms of 1970s feminist art theory and practice and my interest in examining the politics of sexuality (especially the politics of sexuality within feminism itself). These politics are manifest in the debates that have surrounded Judy Chicago's *Dinner Party*, which I would like to position in this catalogue and exhibition as part of the ongoing history of feminist art practice and theory in the United States and Britain.

In order to correct the often simplistic conceptions of early feminist art practice and theory that have been sustained in the celebration and excoriation of *The Dinner Party* as the icon of 1970s feminist art, the exhibition places the piece in the context of a number of other important works from the 1960s to the present which examine the same issues but often in vastly different ways. It will become clear through this juxtaposition that the axis around which the controversy over *The Dinner Party* in particular, and 1970s feminist art in general, has turned is that of female sexuality as the defining component of women's identities and experiences living in patriarchal culture. As *The Dinner Party* makes clear, the exploration and reclaiming of women's sexuality has most often taken place within feminist art practice through the representation or enactment (through performance) of the female body.[2] This project, then, raises fundamental and absolutely contemporary questions about what is at stake in debates over the

political efficacy of the strategies adopted by various generations of feminist artists.[3] The impassioned responses engendered by *The Dinner Party* testify to the importance of these questions—of defining subjectivities and sexualities, of political agency, of women's desires and erotic experiences, of strategies of representation, of how or whether to attempt to define positive female identities, and of what these might be—to ongoing discussions about contemporary culture in general.

More than three years ago I was approached by UCLA with the proposal to exhibit *The Dinner Party*, which has been in storage since its last exhibition, in Melbourne, Australia, in 1988. As an art historian interested in examining and revising

masculinist or otherwise exclusionary histories of culture, I was intrigued by the possibility of showing the piece again (and for the first time in Los Angeles, where it was produced) but felt strongly that this would be useful only if the work were removed from its usual isolation and resituated within the broader context of feminist art practice and theory out of which it developed and within which it has been evaluated. Fascinated by the controversial position *The Dinner Party* has occupied in histories of the contemporary period, I had no idea that this exhibition, in spite of my efforts to work within a historical and theoretical (rather than aesthetic or monographic) framework, would prove as controversial as the piece itself.

While the exhibition foregrounds *The Dinner*

Party itself (that was how it was originally proposed to me, after all), I have tried to articulate this emphasis within a historical framework; this project attempts to explore and critique rather than confirm the reductive image of 1970s feminist art perpetuated by historical accounts that tend to present *The Dinner Party* as the sole or typical exemplar of this diverse movement.[4] While the piece—a monumental table in the form of an equilateral triangular with thirteen place settings on each side, each representing a woman from Western history—asserts itself on such a scale and with such self-assurance that it has tended to marginalize other feminist art from the same period (hence its critique by feminists who find such monumentality problematic), the other feminist works represented here have equal weight in the broader history I am attempting to trace. Nevertheless, *The Dinner Party* has played the most central and controversial (some might say divisive, others heroic) role in debates addressing feminist art practice.

The Dinner Party is thus featured here because of its highly visible role as a catalyst for feminist debate since its premier exhibition, at the San Francisco Museum of Modern Art in 1979. Although (or perhaps because) the work has been controversial, both within feminist circles and in the broader context of the mainstream art world, it has also clearly informed the development of feminist art and theory. At the same time it has not been incorporated in any satisfactory way into histories and theories of feminist or contemporary art; it seems that the very contentiousness of the piece has precluded the thoughtful examination of its effects. Whether adored or abhorred, the piece has tended to be viewed in a vacuum, isolated from its rich historical, artistic, and theoretical contexts. This project begins from the assumption that, like any cultural product, *The Dinner Party* did not spring spontaneously from the mind of one isolated "genius." The piece itself and its cultural effects are a product of years of theorizing, art making, writing, and exhibiting on the part of feminists and other artists, writers, and curators from the 1960s onward. In structuring the show around Chicago's piece and her audacious contributions to feminist pedagogy and to the theorization of feminist imagery, I hope to open up this history to reevaluation.

It is not the purpose of this catalogue or exhibition to recuperate Chicago's piece in a simplistic or unquestioningly celebratory way. Nor is it my aim to join in the general opprobrium in which the piece has been held by many 1980s poststructuralist feminists, who see it as paradigmatic of a naive and putatively "essentialist" arm of 1970s feminist art.[5] Rather, I hope here to look at the piece seriously and with respect for its conflicted but important position—whether as adulated icon of feminist utopianism or despised exemplar of essentialism (the unifying presentation of women's experience as "essential" or biologically determined)—within the history of feminist art.

While I am critical of this particular aspect of poststructuralist feminism, I am at the same time sympathetic to most of the goals of this theoretical movement and, in fact, consider myself a poststructuralist feminist.[6] I am motivated here *not* by a belief that something "true" of the 1970s has been violated and can be rediscovered through "proper" feminist scholarship, but rather by my specifically poststructuralist suspicion of interpretations that pose as "objective" and of the exclusions put into play by the formation of restrictive historical narratives. I am not, then, proposing my writings for this catalogue or the exhibition itself as "true" narratives that replace "false" ones that became predominant in the 1980s but, rather, as ones that, from the more distanced perspective afforded by my position writing in the mid-1990s, offer an alternative, more generous view of feminist art of the 1970s, reinstating some of its complexities and contradictions while respecting the insights of poststructuralism.

The exhibition is organized according to general categories that reflect concerns central to feminist art practice for the last thirty-five years. These categories are not comprehensive (nor is the selection of artists intended to be) but, rather, highlight the issues that have been most controversial in feminist debate over this period, as epitomized by responses to *The Dinner Party*. It could be argued, in fact, that the visibility of Chicago's piece has to do precisely with its flamboyant excess, its pushing of the limits of many of these issues.

The inclusion of studies for *The Dinner Party* as well as works by Chicago that preceded and followed it indicates the importance of these themes and sheds light on their development. The works of other feminists dealing with similar ideas were selected to reveal the broad visual history that has been largely obliterated by the focus on *The Dinner Party* and, in so doing, to highlight the particularities of Chicago's approach. The selection of artists will no doubt appear odd to some, particularly since the controversial nature of this exhibition has prompted five prominent feminist artists—Mary Beth Edelson, Joyce Kozloff, Miriam Schapiro, Joan Snyder, and Nancy Spero—to ask that their works not be included. (Not incidentally, these are among the most established American feminist artists whose work I had hoped to include in the exhibition; they are all more or less of Chicago's generation, and are all based in New York.)[7] I am deeply appreciative of the other artists who may have been equally wary of my approach but who have generously allowed me to borrow their work in order to broaden this historical account.

My essay in this catalogue, "The 'Sexual Politics' of *The Dinner Party*: A Critical Context," explores in some detail the critical and historical positioning of *The Dinner Party* within feminist as well as mainstream modernist and postmodernist art discourse. We will see that the most aggressive feminist critiques (generated primarily by New York and British feminists skeptical of 1970s West Coast or American feminism in general) have focused on the supposedly essentializing vulvar forms of *The Dinner Party* plates (which Chicago developed in consonance with her theory of "central core" imagery); modernist critics have also singled out the plates, labeling them "pornographic" and "kitsch."

The "cunt" images of other feminists (some of which were developed as early as 1960) offer dramatic alternative readings of the essentialism of 1970s American feminist art practice. Thus, Hannah Wilke's early genital objects of 1960–63

and the chewing-gum "sculptures" in her *S.O.S. Starification Object Series*[8] of 1974–82 oscillate between orifice and protrusion, proposing a far more ambiguous and sexually multiplicitous anatomical "destiny" for women (as well as men) than Chicago's central-core images have been interpreted as offering (see figs. 6, 110, cat. nos. 3, 8).[9] Faith Wilding's pulsating *Womb* (1971; fig. 1, cat. no. 6);[10] Maureen Connor's delicate organdy *Bishop's Rose*

FIG. 9
Maureen Connor. *Bishop's Rose*, 1980 (cat. no. 13).

(1980; fig. 9, cat. no. 13); Karen LeCocq's sensual, at once hard and soft *Feather Cunt* (1971; fig. 64, cat. no. 5); and Harmony Hammond's aggressively large-scale but seductive wrapped-fabric oval, *Durango* (1979; fig. 5, cat. no. 12), articulate a subtle and multivalent relationship to the complexities of female sexuality.

Younger artists have explicitly ironicized female anatomy and sexuality, opening the cunt form to multiple desires. Lauren Lesko's playful fur *Lips* (1993; see fig. 10, cat. nos. 17–19) "speak" a woman's sexuality through the sensually pleasurable material of upper-class feminine vanity, and Judie Bamber's meticulously detailed paintings of women's vulvae (see fig. 121, cat. no. 22) explode the conventional equation of women with their sex by giving to the eye all there is to see in such a way that the *differences* among women's sexual organs are

FIG. 10
Lauren Lesko. *Lips*, 1993 (cat. no. 17).

laid bare.[11] Her images—like Tee A. Corinne's explicit but lyrical black-and-white montaged images of women's genitalia (see fig. 7, cat. no. 14) and Millie Wilson's ironic Wigs series (see fig. 2, cat. no. 16), which uses "scientific" images of lesbian genitalia to subvert the historic debasement of lesbian women as medically deviant—solicit polymorphous, and often implicitly female-to-female, viewing pleasures.

While the *Dinner Party* plates arguably lean in the direction of celebrating a universal female identity symbolized by forms evocative of women's bodily experiences, contemporary feminists borrow from this earlier interest in women's sexual experiences but position anatomical signs of femininity as definitively cultural. In two 1993 works Mira Schor employed oil painting, the medium long associated with the masculine privilege of artistic genius, to position both women's and men's anatomical attributes firmly within the realm of culture, symbolizing them with linguistic signifiers that merge into lush, fleshy surfaces (figs. 3–4; cat. nos. 20–21). Marlene McCarty offers a 1990s alternative to central-core imagery, bluntly spelling out the word *cunt* rather than attempting to symbolize it in visual form (see fig. 11, cat. no. 15).

Central-core imagery is one aspect of the broader problematic of "female experience," which has been a locus of exploration in feminist art discourse and practice. A corollary to the early downplaying of differences among women in the drive to form a coalition to combat patriarchy is the assumption that women share particular social, cultural, and personal experiences. In *The Dinner Party*, for example, Chicago created a unified format for representing all thirty-nine women at the table: more or less centralized or specifically vulvar forms on the plates (which, for Chicago, use the metaphor of female sexual power to represent the shared experience of women attempting to gain internal strength to resist the oppression of male-dominated social institutions), surrounded by needlework runners narrating aspects of each woman's life and work.

By making the personal experiences of

women—menstruation, childbearing, maternity, aging, eroticism, domesticity, violence, objectification—political, feminists challenged the age-old erasure of women's participation in Western culture. Chicago's earlier works—such as *Menstruation Bathroom* (1972; fig. 125, cat. no. 24) and *Red Flag* (1971; fig. 24, cat. no. 23)—dramatically uncovered the usually hidden, "impolite" subject of menstruation. Christine Lidrbauch, in contrast, both veils and unveils the materiality of menstrual blood, employing it as "paint" and coding it within the formalist structures of abstraction (see fig. 124, cat. no. 30). Chicago's portrayal of Mary Wollstonecraft giving birth on one of the *Dinner Party* runners and her later *Birth Project* (1980–85; see fig. 103, cat. no. 27) present birth as a heroic yet confining event defining womanhood (although her embroidered image of a mother chained to her baby on the Margaret Sanger runner expresses a more complex, ambivalent view of maternity).

In contrast, Renée Cox, Mary Kelly, Rona Pondick, and Kiki Smith interrogate birth and maternity as *processes* whose personal and cultural meanings, sufferings, and satisfactions are deeply ideological. Kelly's paradigm-shifting *Post-Partum Document* (1974–79; see fig. 28, cat. no. 26), which situates mother-child relations within French psychoanalyst Jacques Lacan's complex model of infant development, moved the terms of feminist art practice away from a positive notion of a femininity unmediated by unconscious processes toward a psychoanalytically based conception of gender as a psychically and culturally inscribed phenomenon. Cox, like Kelly, presents a drastically revised picture of maternity that revolves around its *relational* aspect (as a developmental exchange with the infant or child) rather than idealizing it; her image of a gorgeous, muscular nude black woman nonchalantly cradling a lighter-skinned black child in her arms (fig. 25, cat. no. 31) calls into question the assumption of whiteness underlying Western myths of maternity. Smith's *Womb* (1988; fig. 26, cat. no. 28) ties in to her careerlong interest in the fragility of the body (particularly the female body), especially in the acts of procreation, menstruation, and giving birth.

FIG. 11
Marlene McCarty. *Untitled (CUNT)*, 1990 (cat. no. 15).

Pondick's *No* (1990; fig. 27, cat. no. 29), whose title refers to the "no" that signals infantile independence, explores the paradoxical way in which the mother-child relationship is *culturally* determined as a *natural* process.

Early feminist art theory and practice often took their impetus from the desire to challenge misogynist representations of women as sexual objects in Western art and popular culture, stressing the importance of providing alternative, positive images of women to counter this objectification.[12] Chicago's practice during the 1970s was exemplary of the utopian aspects of this strategy; thus, in *Transformation Painting—Great Ladies Transforming Themselves into Butterflies* (1973; fig. 74; cat. no. 32), she expanded on the centralized, geometric forms of her earlier abstract paintings, developing imagery that clearly evokes female genitalia. She attempted to anchor the meaning of these radiating labial circles through the addition of an extended, handwritten diaristic text that describes the metamorphosis of the abstract forms into more literal representations of women's bodies, describing this transformation as a metaphor for the process of "liberating" oneself from the constraints of patriarchy. The butterfly "liberates" Chicago's earlier Great Ladies abstractions (which, preparing the ground for *The*

LOOKING INTO THE MIRROR, THE BLACK WOMAN ASKED, "MIRROR, MIRROR ON THE WALL, WHO'S THE FINEST OF THEM ALL?" THE MIRROR SAYS, "SNOW WHITE, YOU BLACK BITCH, AND DON'T YOU FORGET IT!!!"

FIG. 12
Carrie Mae Weems. *Mirror, Mirror*, 1986–87 (cat. no. 38).

FIG. 13
Laurie Anderson. *Fully Automated Nikon* (detail), from the series Object, Objection, Objectivity, 1974 (cat. no. 34).

Dinner Party, celebrated notable women in history through centralized forms [see fig. 73, cat. no. 85]), presenting a more explicit expression of feminist ideals.

Chicago's attempt to counter the objectification of women through personal revelation and centralized, abstracted forms contrasts dramatically with contemporaneous critiques by feminists such as Laurie Anderson, Lynn Hershman, and Martha Wilson, all of whom employed a strong sense of irony in their interrogations of the ways in which beauty myths and the male-dominated public sphere objectify women and diminish their sense of themselves as subjects. For these artists, critique itself (rather than celebration) was a form of liberation and empowerment. Anderson's series Object, Objection, Objectivity (1974; see fig. 13, cat. no. 34), a project in which she accosted, photographed, and questioned men who had made sexual comments to her on the street, turns the gaze of desire through which men objectify women back onto the initiating male subjects. Wilson's manipulation of her own image in *I Make Up the Image of My Perfection / I Make Up the Image of My Deformity* (1974; fig. 55, cat. no. 35) and Hershman's *Roberta Breitmore's Construction Chart* (1973; fig. 57, cat. no. 33), which documents her elaborate self-transformation into a fictional female subject, insist upon beauty and femininity themselves as disempowering social constructs.

In the late 1970s and 1980s the majority of feminist artists rejected the celebration of positive images of women in favor of the explicit critique of the objectifying "male gaze" identified by Anderson and others in works from the 1970s.[13] The practices of Sherrie Levine, Barbara Kruger, and Carrie Mae Weems, who appropriate photographs or stage photographic scenarios that expose patriarchal objectification for its ideological effects, exemplify this shift (see figs. 56, 58, 12; cat. nos. 36–38). Playing on the obviously coded myth of Snow White, Weems also points out the racist assumptions implicit in the Western conceptions of beauty that inform representations of women's bodies. In Wilke's last project, Intra-Venus (1992–93; see fig.

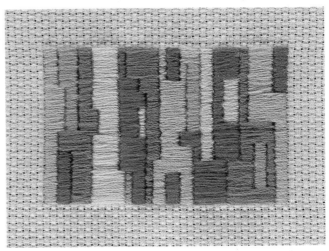

59, cat. no. 39), the artist, who was then dying of cancer, appears nude in poses drawn from traditional representations of the nude both in Western art and in popular magazines such as *Playboy*, brilliantly bringing together the celebratory quality of early 1970s American feminist art and the critical stance that has dominated later works. Even in the midst of her own physical disintegration Wilke insists upon her value (her beauty) as a subject and in so doing throws the very concept of body beautiful into question.

As the recent exhibition *Division of Labor: "Women's Work" in Contemporary Art* showed, feminists from the 1970s to the present have extensively explored domestic themes and techniques, investigating domesticity as a par-

ticular aspect of female experience.[14] Louise Bourgeois has been a pioneer of feminist art, as her *Femme Maison* series, completed just after World War II, attests. Artfully merging the female body with the house itself, Bourgeois set the stage for Betty Friedan's exposure of the downside to the domestic ideal of femininity fifteen years later in *The Feminine Mystique*. One of the central goals of *The Dinner Party*, which foregrounds "feminine" techniques (embroidery, ceramics, china painting), was to confront the public domain of high art (the province of men, who empower themselves by excluding women's culture as low art or craft) with the private realm of domesticity (conventionally assigned to women). Chicago's expertise in china painting, which she developed through intensive study with women

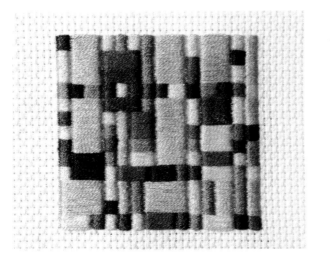

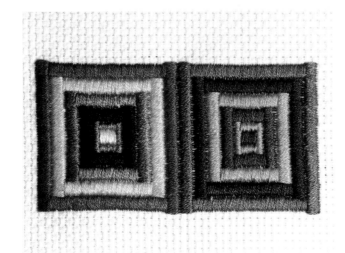

FIG. 14 (TOP)
Judy Chicago.
Butterfly Test Plate #4, 1973/74
(cat. no. 47).

FIGS. 15–17
(CLOCKWISE FROM TOP LEFT)
Didi Dunphy. *Modernist
Samplers*, 1995 (cat nos. 58–60).

"master" china painters, was put to use early on in her series of erotic "buttons" or butterflies (1974; figs. 84–87, cat. nos. 52–55), which explicitly *sexualize* the domestic technique of china painting with highly charged, erotic imagery (just as Sherry Brody's Lingerie Pillows [figs. 77–80, cat. nos. 41–43] playfully conflate the pillow, a benign, obliquely maternal object of domestic comfort, with the charged eroticism of silk lingerie).

In real-time performances that dramatize the boredom and exhaustion of domestic and institutional labor, Sandra Orgel and Mierle Laderman Ukeles performed maintenance tasks (see figs. 81–82, 146; cat. nos. 40, 45, 51).[15] Like Chicago, Didi Dunphy, Harmony Hammond, Joyce Kozloff, Faith Ringgold, Betye Saar, and Miriam Schapiro have employed techniques and objects associated with the home. A cross between home decoration and abstract painting, Hammond's radiating *Floor-*

FIG. 18
Cindy Sherman. *Untitled Film Still #35,* 1979 (cat. no. 56).

pieces (see figs. 75, 137–38; cat. nos. 48–50) and Dunphy's tiny needlepoint "canvases" (see figs. 15–17, cat. nos. 58–60) force an intersection between the "low" forms of women's culture and the "high" forms of modernism. Dunphy's use of needlework to produce controlled modernist patterns contrasts markedly with the more illustrative imagery of *The Dinner Party* runners.

Closer to these runners in decorative effect are the works of Kozloff, Ringgold, and Schapiro, who use needle and fabric crafts in picturesque or seminarrative ways. For Ringgold, who combines quilting techniques with painting, the aim is not only to place women within history but also to give black women and men a central place in cultural narratives, as exemplified in her *Woman Painting the Bay Bridge* (1988; fig. 76, cat. no. 57).

Saar takes actual household materials and recontextualizes them in a critical way. Her *Liberation of Aunt Jemima* (1972; fig. 19, cat. no. 46) acerbically recalls the association of domesticity not just with women in general but also with the African American women who spent their lives trapped in this narrow sphere of productivity as slaves and maids. Staging herself within a corny domestic scene, Cindy Sherman, an artist who has come to be closely associated with poststructuralist (or postmodern) feminism, eschews the use of actual household materials, exploiting the documentary pretensions of black-and-white photography to subvert the authority of popular images of women as happy homemakers (see fig. 18, cat. no. 56).

The rage that motivated Chicago to devote her life as an artist to challenging the exclusion of women from history and from art institutions—expressed in her *Female Rejection Drawing* (1974; fig. 68, cat. no. 65) and her *Love Story* (1970; fig. 20, cat. no. 62), which uses the text-image technique associated with 1980s feminist practice to voice an urgent protest against violence toward women—has also driven a number of women who have attacked more specifically the literal acts of violence to which women have

FIG. 19 (OPPOSITE)
Betye Saar. *The Liberation of Aunt Jemima,* 1972 (cat. no. 46).

self-fashioning as the striding, jubilant Virgin of Guadalupe, a revered figure in Catholicized Latino culture (1978; fig. 129, cat. no. 82), to Rachel Rosenthal's theatrical explorations of the rise and fall of matriarchy and goddess culture in *Gaia Mon Amour* (1984; fig. 132, cat. no. 83).

Rather than dealing with historical narrative directly, some feminists have approached the dilemma of women's exclusion from Western culture by parodying or otherwise critiquing male power. Adopting pugilist's garb in her 1970 advertisement in *Artforum* (fig. 35, cat. no. 84), Chicago facetiously presented herself as "one of the boys," ready to come out fighting for women's art, while Lynda Benglis's infamous *Artforum* advertisement (1974; fig. 147, cat. no. 87) endows the artist with an obviously fake "phallus" of artistic and cultural authority. In her Powerplay series (including the 1984 *Disfigured by Power 2* [fig. 149, cat. no. 89]), as in *The Dinner Party*, Chicago interrogates patriarchy through crudely expressive, yet subtly colored and modulated, figures. This series exemplifies her efforts, in *The Dinner Party* and succeeding works, to narrate a feminist polemic in increasingly explicit terms. Judith Bernstein, known for her huge paintings of penislike screws, and Carole Caroompas, a Los Angeles feminist who employs hieratic patterns and decorative motifs with startlingly direct sexual imagery, dramatize in a humorous way the alignment of the anatomical penis with this empowering phallus (see figs. 151–52; cat. nos. 86, 91). Karen Finley, in her installation *Moral History* (1994; fig. 150, cat. no. 92), also interrogates the assumptions underlying art historical value systems. Placing art magazines and books under a sheet of plate glass, Finley challenges their privileging of male genius by writing negative comments about the texts' heroizing of male artists and objectification of women in an aggressive red pen on the glass.

Perhaps the most insistent critiques of 1970s feminism, and the most convincing criticisms of *The Dinner Party* itself, have been articulated by women suspicious of the ways in which mainstream feminism (which Chicago has been seen as epitomizing) has tended to assume a unified womanhood that, in fact, is implicitly white, heterosexual, and middle or upper-middle class. As I discuss at length in my essay here, although Chicago included lesbians (Sappho, Natalie Barney, Virginia Woolf) and nonwhite women (Hatshepsut, Sacagawea, Sojourner Truth) at the *Dinner Party* table, she was reluctant to foreground differences among women, and *The Dinner Party* has been seen as falling short in giving full representation to other aspects of "female experience." While some feminists, especially women of color and lesbians, debated at length the issues of race and sexual orientation in the 1970s, these were often implicitly marginalized by feminists such as Chicago, who saw as paramount the formation of a unified coalition of women to fight patriarchy. At the time, because of the pressing need to articulate a cohesive feminist point of view, women's oppression was generally viewed (especially by white feminists) in isolation from other discriminatory structures, such as racism.

Adrian Piper and Eleanor Antin were unusual in that they countered the myth of a unified female experience early in the 1970s through performances that questioned the fixity of women's experience in racial terms (see figs. 23, 157; cat. nos. 93, 98). Making it clear that race was not ignored in the 1970s, Sheila Levrant de Bretteville's 1977 design for the cover of *Chrysalis* (fig. 71, cat. no. 94) dramatized the heterogeneity of women as a group.[21] More recently many younger feminists of color and lesbian feminists have insistently opened feminism to multiple points of view, multiple women's desires and experiences. In Laura Aguilar's powerful parody of the odalisque—*In Sandy's Room (Self-Portrait)* (1991; fig. 156, cat. no. 99)—the artist's own *zaftig* Latina body is substituted for that of Manet's Olympia. Catherine Opie's series of portraits of "deviant" women and men features a diverse group of subjects who cross over a range of sexual, gender, racial, and class identities.

Opie's *Dyke* (1992; fig. 144, cat. no. 100) is a far cry from Chicago's glowingly complete image of lesbian identity in the Natalie Barney place setting of *The Dinner Party* (fig. 45), just as Wilke's hermaphroditic body parts provide an interesting counterargument to the muscular labial forms of the *Dinner Party* plates. Likewise, Saar's *Liberation of Aunt Jemima* points to a more specific site of oppression in the domestic arena than Chicago's exploration, with collaborator Susan Hill, of the decorative and narrative possibilities of embroidery in the *Dinner Party* runners. All of these works inform one another in evocative ways and begin to suggest why *The Dinner Party*, with its exuberant excessiveness and ambitious program, has become such a contentious monument in discussions of contemporary feminist art.

The essays in this catalogue, all written by young feminist critics and scholars who offer a fresh take on the trajectory of feminist art theory and practice over the last two decades, address the problematic position held by *The Dinner Party* in contemporary (especially feminist) art discourse from a variety of perspectives. Laura Meyer's essay examines the relationship of *The Dinner Party* to Chicago's prior work and to the complex history of the feminist art movement in early 1970s Southern California, as well as to the earlier Los Angeles finish fetish movement of the 1960s (in which Chicago was virtually the only female participant). Through her analysis Meyer complicates the tendency to view *The Dinner Party* as a work that sprang solely from Chicago's commitment to feminism or as a unique expression generated in isolation. Chicago's pedagogical goals and experiences are linked to her role as "master" of the *Dinner Party* studio, and the works of her numerous colleagues and students from this earlier period are discussed.

My essay, as noted, is a historical study of the critical reception of *The Dinner Party* which attempts to surface what has been at stake in feminist and modernist or postmodernist discourses that have defined it negatively as the icon of a particular period of feminist practice. The criticisms leveled at the piece—that it is essentialist, that it is kitsch, that it is pornographic, that it reinforces masculinist notions of greatness, that it betrays the feminist commitment to collaboration, that it is too populist, and so on—raise issues that are central to feminist practice. By examining critiques of the work from the popular press, art journals, feminist magazines, and articles and books on feminist art history and theory, I attempt to return it as fully as possible to the complex history of feminism in the visual arts.

Nancy Ring's "Identifying with Judy Chicago"

departs from conventional scholarly discourse to unhinge the transcendent values ascribed to Chicago's work, by the artist herself as well as by historians and critics. Ring extends the feminist strategy of marking the political aspects of the personal by projecting her own highly specific identifications onto aspects of Chicago's life history, imposing particularity onto the universalizing identity politics she sees inscribed in *The Dinner Party*. In her engagement with Chicago, Ring highlights Chicago's Jewishness, which was largely buried at the time of *The Dinner Party*'s creation (it emerged forcefully only with the artist's recent *Holocaust Project*, completed in collaboration with her husband, Donald Woodman). Ring reads *The Dinner Party* through the lens of Chicago's Jewishness, problematizing the artist's attempted projection of a unified female experience.

Expanding on this contextualization, Anette Kubitza takes a historical approach in her analysis of the reception of *The Dinner Party* in Great Britain and Germany. She resituates the generally hostile responses to the piece within a broader context of ideological struggle within feminist art discourse and practice in these two countries, highlighting the geographical as well as generational politics within feminist debate. In demonstrating how *The Dinner Party* has meant many different things to many different people according to their varying approaches to feminist art practice, Kubitza reveals how the piece has generated and participated in a critical discourse that goes far beyond Chicago's particular aesthetic and political concerns.

Susan Kandel's "Beneath the Green Veil" takes up the focused language of art criticism to explore and critique the feminist search for the "elusive truth of the female body." Pointing out that pornographers have a similar aim, Kandel relates this search to Chicago's conceptualization of the centralized form as a repository of female sexual experience. She compares Chicago's approach with more recent explorations of the female sex by feminist artists. She argues that artists who emerged in the late 1980s and 1990s, such as Zoe Leonard, Christine Lidrbauch, Kiki

Smith, and Jana Sterbak, have rendered the female body as definitively social rather than "essential," effectively countering the search for truth that Kandel aligns with Chicago's project.

In "Eating from the Dinner Party Plates and Other Myths, Metaphors, and Moments of Lesbian Enunciation in Feminism and Its Art Movement," Laura Cottingham attempts to render feminism more complex. Her polemical attack on the heterosexism of feminist art discourse explores the ways in which lesbian feminist artists have had to negotiate these exclusions within feminism itself as well as the culture at large. Cottingham's positing of lesbianism as a determinable identity with its own identifiable creative codes allies her argument with Chicago's labial dinner plates.

The numerous works by feminist artists of color in the exhibition attest to the centrality of the voices of nonwhite women to feminist practice over the last three decades. A notable absence in this catalogue is an essay written by a woman of color who might address firsthand the exclusions put into play by particular aspects of 1970s (and subsequent) feminist art practice. This absence is strategic, however, in that it reflects the specificity of the debates over *The Dinner Party*, which have been articulated almost exclusively by white feminists from the United States and Britain. Nancy Ring's surfacing of Chicago's Jewishness begins to expose the heterogeneity of whiteness and thus to challenge the blindness of much feminist theory and practice to the issue of racial and ethnic difference.

By and large, with the exception of Lorraine O'Grady and writer Alice Walker, women of color have paid no attention to *The Dinner Party*. The question of why so few feminists of color have evinced any interest in the piece or the issues it has raised is one that merits further study. The problem of essentialism has been obsessively debated by white feminists, who seem to have less to lose in exploring their own sexu-

ality in public than do women of color. The issues of collaboration, populism, and artistic authority have a completely different resonance for feminists of color, who have little interest in combatting formalism (a mode of discourse specific to white privilege), exposing their bodies within their work, or relinquishing artistic authority. As O'Grady has observed, black women artists have rarely portrayed nude black women in their work, much less black women's genitalia: "When even the black woman's ability to survive being raped 'proved' she was less than human (a real woman would have committed suicide rather than submit), was it any wonder that black artists wanted, not to take her clothes off, but to keep them on?"[22]

Finally, I hope that this show will contribute to the historicization of feminist art. Positioning *The Dinner Party* within the complex history of its reception and placing it for the first time among other feminist works, the exhibition attempts to reopen now-reified debates about feminist practice. While perhaps inevitably flawed as a curatorial project by the dominance of the piece itself (a dominance that underlines its contentious but undeniably important position in feminist and contemporary art histories), *Sexual Politics* should at least encourage us to question the reasons for the almost automatic dismissal of *The Dinner Party* by modernists, postmodernists, and many feminists alike, as well as the corollary assumption that it represents in totality the rich work from this period. From Bourgeois's mid-1940s Femme Maison to Aguilar's 1991 self-portrait and Bamber's explicit 1994 paintings of vulvae (with *The Dinner Party* wedged somewhere in between), the problematic of women's experience in patriarchy (and, indeed, of how we might define *women*) has been central to feminist practice and has transformed the ways art is made and discussed in contemporary culture. The extreme responses that *The Dinner Party* has aroused are reason enough for its thoughtful reevaluation; it is my hope that this exhibition and catalogue will initiate a reexamination and open the way for a more nuanced understanding of the "sexual politics" of feminist art.

Notes

1. Kate Millett, *Sexual Politics* (Garden City, N.Y.: Doubleday, 1970), 24–25. Flora Davis discusses the importance of this book to the feminist movement in *Moving the Mountain: The Women's Movement in America since 1960* (New York: Simon and Schuster, 1991), 116. Although I clearly diverge from Millett in important respects, I have chosen to use this 1970s locution for historical and theoretical reasons; furthermore, Millett is an important feminist artist in her own right, and so her argument has a doubly appropriate place in this history. While working on *Sexual Politics*, in fact, Millett designed a prototype for disposable dinnerware that prefigured aspects of Chicago's *Dinner Party* (see fig. 134). See Kristine Stiles, "Between Water and Stone—Fluxus Performance: A Metaphysics of Acts," in *In the Spirit of Fluxus*, ed. Elizabeth Armstrong and Joan Rothfuss (Minneapolis: Walker Art Center, 1993), 79.

2. As I explore in my forthcoming book on body art, *Performing the Subject* (University of Minnesota Press), feminist performance in particular has worked to dissolve the boundaries between woman as sexual object and woman as sexual (and art-making) subject.

3. I use the term *feminist* loosely to describe artists who in some way attempt to revalue women as creative subjects or to critique aspects of patriarchy in their work.

4. While recent editions of the major historical surveys of Western art have expanded to include other work by feminist artists, earlier editions, if they showed any feminist works at all, tended to show only *The Dinner Party*.

5. A diverse body of critical ideas spearheaded by British art historians such as Griselda Pollock and Lisa Tickner which rose to prominence in the late 1970s and 1980s, poststructuralist feminism draws on psychoanalysis, theories of representation developed in film studies and literary criticism, and Marxian theories of ideology.

6. This allegiance differentiates me from other supporters of the work of Chicago and other American feminist artists of the 1970s, such as Norma Broude and Mary Garrard, who have attempted to revalue 1970s feminist practice but at the expense of what they perceive as "phallic" theory (this is actually Chicago's term; see Norma Broude and Mary D. Garrard, "Conversation with Judy Chicago," in *The Power of Feminist Art: The American Movement of the 1970s, History and Impact*, ed. Norma Broude and Mary D. Garrard [New York: Harry N. Abrams, 1994], 66–73). Broude and Garrard dismiss "theory" (i.e., poststructuralism) in what I view to be an ill-informed way in their introduction to this volume; see esp. 28–29. I explore in more detail the tension between poststructuralists and supporters of 1970s American feminism in my review of this book, "Power and Feminist Art (History)," *Art History* 18 (September 1995): 435–43.

7. Several artists objected to the show because they saw it as reinforcing what they perceive to be the heroization of Chicago. I address the personality politics at stake in such perceptions in my essay in this catalogue. Chicago has been supportive but has not intervened in the organization of the show or the catalogue; I hope this introduction will dispel the misapprehension of both as having been in some way directed by Chicago.

8. The loops of gum that form grid patterns in the *S.O.S. Starification Object Series* resemble both labia and the glans of a penis. Wilke stated that "from a woman's point of view" each "bubblegum cunt" looks like the "head of a cock" ("Artist Hannah Wilke Talks with Ernst," *Oasis de Neon* 1, no. 1 [1978], n.p.).

9. The reference here is to Sigmund Freud's infamous statement that "anatomy is destiny." Wilke deeply disliked *The Dinner Party*, arguing that "By labeling a woman as a vagina . . . the piece [is] denigrating to women" (cited in Susan Paul, "The Just Desserts: 'Dinner Party,' Now Closed, Draws Praise and Attack," *The Phoenix*, 12 February 1981, 19). I am grateful to Donald Goddard for pointing out this reference to me.

10. Wilding, still a feminist activist, writer, and artist, was working with Chicago in the Fresno Feminist Art Program when she made this piece.

11. I have pointed out elsewhere that Bamber's cunts vary widely in size, proportions, and skin texture but all appear to be Anglo in race ("Judie Bamber," *Artforum* 33 [October 1994]: 108–9).

12. Griselda Pollock, whose work is discussed more fully in my essay in this catalogue, "The 'Sexual Politics' of *The Dinner Party*," went on record early on as opposing such strategies. See her "What's Wrong with Images of Women?" *Screen Education*, no. 24 (Autumn 1977): 25–33.

13. This move toward a concern with dislocating the "male gaze," as I note in my essay, was informed by poststructuralist models of signification and gender development proposed by feminists working primarily in Britain, such as Pollock (and including Mary Kelly, who is from the United States but worked in London in the 1970s). Laura Mulvey's well-known essay "Visual Pleasure and Narrative Cinema" (originally published in *Screen* in 1975) was, like Kelly's *Post-Partum Document*, a crucial element in the shift toward poststructuralist feminist models of critique. In the essay Mulvey argues that the central feminist project should be a critique of structures of male pleasure (reprinted in *Visual and Other Pleasures* [Bloomington: Indiana University Press, 1989], 14–26).

14. See *Division of Labor: "Women's Work" in Contemporary Art*, exh. cat. (Bronx, N.Y.: Bronx Museum of the Arts, 1995).

15. Orgel's 1972 *Ironing* performance was part of Womanhouse, an actual house transformed by Chicago and her students and colleagues from the Feminist Art Program into a feminist environment; see Laura Meyer's essay in this volume.

16. Lacy, sometimes in collaboration, has completed a number of projects addressing violence toward women. These include *Rape Is . . .* , a book project completed in 1972, and *Three Weeks in May* (1977), an extensive series of collaborative performance events staged throughout Los Angeles. Lacy was a student and teaching assistant in Chicago's Feminist Art Program. See Moira Roth, "Suzanne Lacy: Social Reformer and Witch," *TDR* 32 (Spring 1988): 42–60, and Chicago's description of *Ablutions* in *Through the Flower: My Struggle as a Woman Artist* (New York: Penguin Books, 1975), 217–19.

17. See *Howardena Pindell: Paintings and Drawings: A Retrospective Exhibition, 1972–1992*, exh. cat. (Potsdam: Roland Gibson Gallery, Potsdam College of the State University of New York, 1992), 60–61.

18. Semmel is quoted in Dorothy Seiberling, "The Female View of Erotica," *New York*, 11 February 1974, 55. Wayne was an influential figure on the Southern Californian art scene in the 1970s, originating a series of "Joan of Art" lectures with the aim of empowering women artists by teaching them how to promote, document, and produce their work in a male-dominated culture. See Faith Wilding, *By Our Own Hands: The Women Artists' Movement, Southern California, 1970–1976* (Santa Monica, Calif.: Double X, 1977), 22–23.

19. Lorraine O'Grady, "Artist Statement," 15 June 1995; see also her "Olympia's Maid: Reclaiming Black Female Subjectivity," in *New Feminist Criticism: Art, Identity, Action*, ed. Joanna Frueh, Cassandra Langer, and Arlene Raven (New York: Harper Collins, 1994), 152–70. I am indebted to O'Grady for sharing her views with me.

20. See Faith Ringgold, *The French Collection*, pt. 1 (New York: Being My Own Woman Press, 1992); Moira Roth introduced this work to me.

21. De Bretteville led the design portion of the Feminist Art Program at the California Institute of the Arts and designed Chicago's two original *Dinner Party* books: *The Dinner Party: A Symbol of Our Heritage* (Garden City, N.Y.: Doubleday, 1979) and *Embroidering Our Heritage: The Dinner Party Needlework* (Garden City, N.Y.: Doubleday, 1980).

22. Lorraine O'Grady, "On Being the Presence That Signals an Absence," unpublished paper, 1993.

"I think it's a waste

of energy to [argue about whether gender is biological or cultural]. . . . Of course, femininity is a construct and masculinity is a construct. I certainly think most gender differences are cultural, but there's also some intersection between culture and biology."

—Judy Chicago

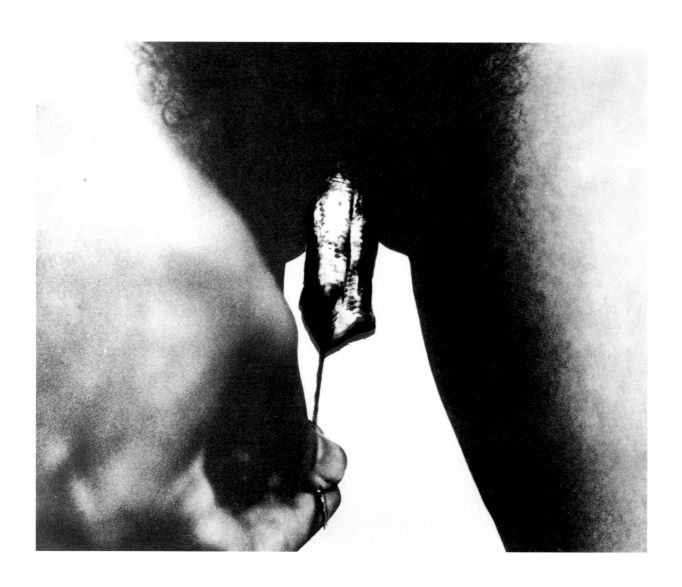

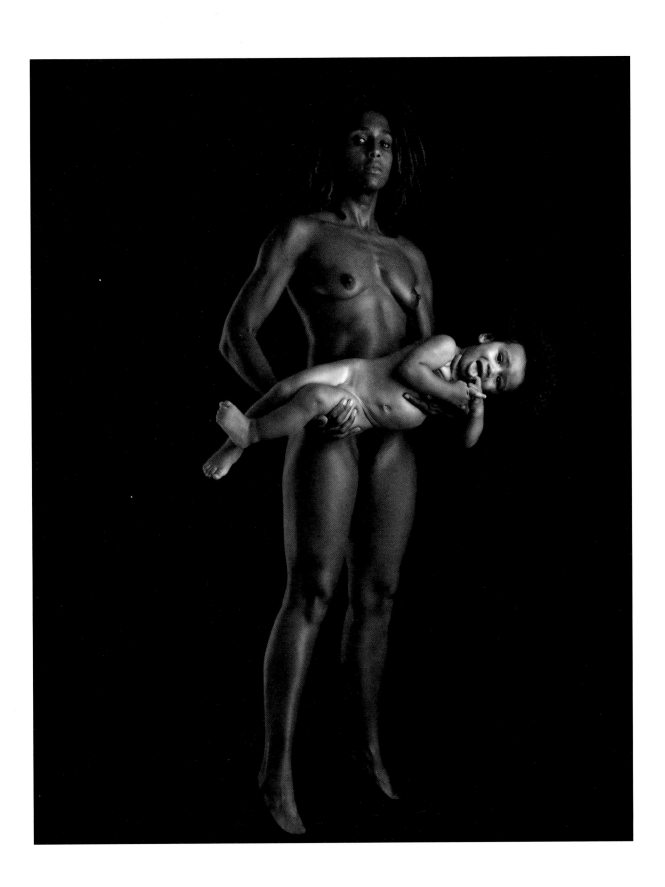

FIG. 25
Renée Cox. *Yo Mama*, 1993 (cat. no. 31).

FIG. 26
Kiki Smith. *Womb*, 1988 (cat. no. 28).

Laura Meyer

As one of the most ambitious and best-known works to emerge from the feminist art movement of the 1970s, Judy Chicago's *Dinner Party* has been the focus of intense controversy. It has elicited adulation from a wide audience of mostly female viewers and drawn condemnation from conservative art critics and politicians as well as a new generation of feminist theorists. Many of those who saw the piece when it was first shown, in 1979 and the early 1980s, found dramatic affirmation in its emphasis on female sexuality and on women's achievements, a message that resonated with the goals of the feminist movement at that time. Art critics, however, have tended to view *The Dinner Party* as an anomaly divorced from the history of art, dismissing it as "kitsch" or "sociology."[1] More recently, right-wing politicians and feminist writers have joined in the criticism of *The Dinner Party*, the former charging that the work's sexual imagery is pornographic, the latter expressing concern that such imagery reinforces body-based sexual stereotypes.[2]

Previous discussions of *The Dinner Party* have neglected the history of Chicago's artistic development within the Los Angeles art world of the 1950s and 1960s, and her subsequent involvement in the 1970s with the feminist art movement in California. *The Dinner Party* marks the intersection of two important developments that have themselves been underrepresented in contemporary histories of art: the so-called finish fetish movement of the early 1960s, which distinguished Los Angeles as an art center of international importance, and the pioneering feminist art education program that Chicago established at Fresno State College in 1970 and later, in collaboration with

Miriam Schapiro, moved to the California Institute of the Arts (CalArts).

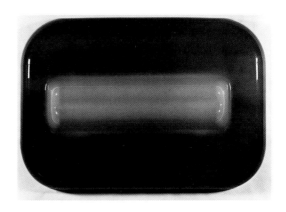

The Dinner Party synthesizes the cool technical perfection of finish fetish with the heated demands of the early feminist movement. It counters the worship of technology in post–World War II society with a painstaking tribute to traditional women's handiwork. It calls into question the sexual norms imposed by society on both women and men. By freeing *The Dinner Party* from its critical isolation and restoring it to art historical discourse, we can gain a richer understanding of both the artwork itself and the conflict-ridden historical period in which it was produced.

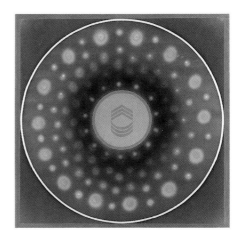

Judy Gerowitz and "The Studs"

Judy Chicago came of age as an artist during the Los Angeles art boom of the late 1950s and 1960s, a circumstance that has had lasting repercussions over the course of her career. In 1957 the daughter of Jewish radicals then known as Judy Cohen decided to leave her hometown of Chicago to attend art school at the University of California, Los Angeles (UCLA). That spring the now-legendary Ferus Gallery, the city's first professional gallery dedicated primarily to the exhibition of avant-garde work by local artists, was founded by artist Edward Kienholz and curator Walter Hopps. In the course of its ten-year existence the gallery defined and promoted a unique Los Angeles aesthetic, known internationally as the "L.A. look," the "cool school," or, most frequently, as "finish fetish." Chicago's undergraduate and graduate studies at UCLA thus

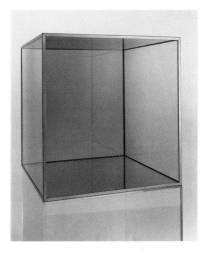

FIGS. 30–33 (FROM TOP)

Craig Kauffman (b. Eagle Rock, California, 1932). *Untitled Wall Relief*, 1967; vacuum-formed Plexiglas; 72 x 50 x 15 in. Los Angeles County Museum of Art, gift of the Kleiner Foundation.

Larry Bell (b. Chicago 1939). *Untitled*, 1968; coated glass; 18 x 18 x 18 in. Courtesy of the artist and Kiyo Higashi Gallery, Los Angeles.

Billy Al Bengston (b. Dodge City, Kansas, 1934). *Buster*, 1962; oil and sprayed lacquer on Masonite; 60 x 60 in. Museum of Contemporary Art, San Diego.

Kenneth Price (b. Los Angeles 1935). *S. Violet*, 1963; fired and painted clay; 70 x 11 in. with pedestal. Collection of Mrs. and Mr. Donn Chappellet.

FIG. 34

Ferus Gallery exhibition announcement featuring John Altoon, Craig Kauffman, Allen Lynch, Edward Kienholz, Ed Moses, Robert Irwin, and Billy Al Bengston, 1959. Photograph by Patricia Faure.

coincided with the development in Los Angeles, for the first time in the city's history, of a cohesive local avant-garde art scene that attracted national and international acclaim.

While the earliest exhibitions at Ferus Gallery featured mainly Northern and Southern California abstract expressionism and assemblage, the gallery rapidly became known for its unique, distinctively "cool" aesthetic, emphasizing the clean lines, surface perfection, and sensuous optical effects made possible by contemporary industrial techniques. As a critical supplier of military equipment during World War II and the Korean and Vietnam Wars, as well as an important hub of the growing aerospace industry, Los Angeles was home to the development of a number of new petrochemical plastics, including acrylic (known commercially as Plexiglas or Lucite), vinyl, and polyester. These modern materials soon found applications in the local consumer culture—in the form of shiny surfboard and boat finishes and automobile and motorcycle lacquers—and were eventually used to create art. The various

currents of the new Los Angeles aesthetic promoted by Ferus and other local galleries were united by the exploitation of these high-tech materials, which were equally evocative of military and technological prowess and Southern California sunshine and speed.[3]

Among the pioneers of finish fetish was Billy Al Bengston, a serious surfer and motorcycle racer who began in 1960 and 1961 to apply the spray-paint techniques and materials used in motorcycle repair to his artwork. Carefully built up with as many as thirty layers of sprayed translucent lacquer on Masonite or aluminum, Bengston's concentrically organized rings, ovals, and squares orbit around a crisply outlined central emblem, usually his trademark sergeant's stripes, to create a mesmerizing force field of indeterminate space (see fig. 32). The resulting tension between the paintings' emotionally evocative atmospheric effects and their industrial method of manufacture is one that pervades the work of the finish fetish artists. The youngest of the group, Larry Bell, who joined Ferus in 1962 at the age of twenty-three, extended Bengston's experiments with absorbed and reflected light in a series of transparent and translucent cubes, constructed of heavy sheets of glass that he vacuum-coated with anodized particles of metal, joined with channels of polished chrome, and displayed on transparent glass or plastic stands to encourage the free circulation of light (see fig. 31).[4] Craig Kauffman experimented with shockingly brilliant translucent and opaque acrylic lacquers, spray-painted on the reverse surfaces of monumental vacuum-molded plastic bubbles or "erotic thermometers."[5] Ambient light penetrating these quasi-organic forms mingles and shifts color according to the viewer's movements (see fig. 30). A particularly disconcerting confrontation between nature and culture was effected by Kenneth Price's ceramic "eggs," whose pristine, candy-colored shells, glazed with automobile lacquer, are marred by cavities from which dark, elemental larval or germinal forms protrude (see fig. 33).

Contemporary critics writing about finish fetish art placed great emphasis on the work's ob-

FIG. 39

Feminist Art Program, California Institute of the Arts. *The Dining Room*, 1972; mixed-media installation at Womanhouse, Los Angeles.

Locating sexual issues within the larger context of human identity, intimacy, and power, the students often confronted violence against women with equally violent imagery. A local slaughterhouse provided materials for Wilding's 1970 *Sacrifice* (fig. 38), in which a deathly-pale wax effigy of the artist lay before an altar heaped with bloody, decaying cow intestines. Facing a white cross erected before a wall of blood-soaked sanitary napkins, *Sacrifice* suggests that the shame projected onto menstruation plays a near-religious role in patriarchal society, sacrificing women's dignity for the illusionistic "purity" of others. Chicago's *Menstruation Bathroom* (fig. 125, cat. no. 24), an environment staged for the CalArts Feminist Art Program's Womanhouse installation in 1972, further expanded on this menstruation imagery. The *Bathroom*'s pristine white shelves are filled to overflowing with various commercial products designed to conceal the "embar-rassing" signs of menstruation, but these products prove powerless to stop the flow of blood that seems to spill angrily from a nearby basket of red-stained sanitary napkins. *Ablutions* (see fig. 96, cat. no. 63), a piece written by Chicago, Suzanne Lacy, Sandra Orgel, and Aviva Rahmani for Chicago's performance workshop at CalArts in 1972, was one of the first public presentations to address the subject of rape. Accompanied by a recording of women's voices describing their experiences of rape, the naked performers were bathed in eggs, blood, and clay and then ritually bound, in a cathartic reenactment of violence and constriction.[36]

Chicago was known as an extremely demanding teacher who required long working hours and total commitment from her students.[37] Rather than leading traditional lecture classes and critiques, she required students to share fusing of form with content, emphasizing that her choice of media was linked to the social and psychological content of the work.[48]

At the same time she began studying china painting, Chicago was searching for a clearly readable means of expressing sexual content in abstract artwork. Consciously putting her central-core theory into practice, she began work on a series of anatomically based paintings and drawings organized around a central opening or focal point. In the earliest of these works, *Through the Flower* (1973; fig. 43, cat. no. 7; Chicago later gave the same title to her autobiography), she created a floral image with strong, red-orange petals opening onto a radiant blue-green center. The painting seemingly offers a vision from *within* the vagina onto a celestial field of light, an image of birth that simultaneously implies a path to "enlightenment" by way of the flesh. *Let It All Hang Out* (1973; fig. 44), created for *Female Sexuality / Female Identity*, the inaugural exhibition of the Los Angeles cooperative gallery Womanspace, is an even more explicitly sexual image, composed of pulsating rings of pink and violet paint, which evoke the contractions of orgasm.[49] Both paintings stand in direct contrast to Chicago's ironic *Heaven Is for White Men Only* (1973), in which crossed cylindrical forms appear to bar access to a central, light-filled space.

Chicago personalized the central-core image in two series of abstract "portraits" dedicated to specific historical personages. In Great Ladies (1972–73; see fig. 73, cat. no. 85) and the Reincarnation Triptych (1973) female monarchs and intellectuals, respectively, are represented by a radiant central-core image enclosed in a band of handwritten text. The didactic text expresses Chicago's ideas about the honored women's lives and imagined feelings.[50]

Female Rejection Drawing (fig. 68, cat. no. 65), from the Rejection Quintet of 1974, is the most blatantly autobiographical and doggedly literal-minded of the central-core paintings. The image shows the now-familiar rays of Chicago's radiant central-core icon literally peeling away from the surface of the painting to reveal the folds

and crevices of a woman's vulva. An extended text accompanying the drawing details Chicago's own fears and dreams as a woman artist. Reiterating its message on three levels of representation—the abstract central-core image, the more explicit vulvar image, and the even more explicit text—*Female Rejection Drawing* demands to be understood on the artist's terms. Female sexuality is pictured as a locus of vulnerability and power, from which women's creative energy flows.

FIG. 44
Judy Chicago. *Let It All Hang Out*, 1973; sprayed acrylic on canvas; 80 x 80 in. Through the Flower, Santa Fe, New Mexico.

Chicago soon began combining ceramic painting with sexual imagery in a series of experiments that eventually expanded from two-inch porcelain knobs to the fourteen-inch *Dinner Party* plates. The thirty Porcelain Miniatures of 1974 (see fig. 50) are tiny, precious fetishes, mounted on six-by-six-inch porcelain tiles and encased in velvet-lined boxes. The handwritten script encircling each knob is as precise and unremarkable as a schoolmarm's, its innocuous appearance belying the imaginative force of the content expressed therein. According to the artist, the Porcelain Miniatures transform the female sexual organs into "every possible thing the vagina [can] become . . . the vagina as temple, tomb, cave, or flower, [or] the Butterfly Vagina which gets

FIG. 45

Judy Chicago. *Natalie Barney Place Setting*, from *The Dinner Party*, 1979 (cat. no. 1).

FIG. 46

Judy Chicago. *Caroline Herschel Runner*, from *The Dinner Party*, 1979 (cat. no. 1); wool, linen, silk thread; 56 x 30 in.

to be an active vaginal form."[51]

In *Flesh Spreading Her Wings and Preparing to Fly* (fig. 50), a central vulvar-vegetal pod is encircled by rippling pink folds, divided into four separate "wings" like those of a butterfly, but suggesting as well the striations of human muscle tissue. This is not "inert flesh painted by a male painter, but an

FIG. 47

Judy Chicago. *Emily Dickinson Plate*, from *The Dinner Party*, 1979 (cat. no. 1); china paint on porcelain; diam: 14 in.

active form—about to fly."[52] *Sex from the Inside Out* (1975; fig. 48, cat. no. 70) is a disarming little diorama composed of six clitoral ceramic knobs encircled by primly scripted instructions from a woman to her lover: "[1] Enter me slowly and gently, she said, [2] Just rub it around in there for a while, [3] Hold still and let me move around on it, [4] There, there, that's the place that feels good, [5] Now, push it all the way up in there, [6] And draw my orgasm right down on you."[53]

By 1974 Chicago had revised her original plan to paint one hundred "Great Ladies" on porcelain plates and determined instead to "work on smaller projects[!]—the first one will be called *The Dinner*

Party." Initially conceived as a table set for twenty-five historical figures, *The Dinner Party* was to combine "images of *traditional* women (symbolized by china painters) with *radical* women (represented by those who were politically active) at each place setting."[54] Vacillating between the desire to make the point that women have been "consumed by history" and a conflicting wish to present women who could be "models for the future," Chicago ultimately determined to undertake an ambitious symbolic history of women in Western civilization, beginning with a mythological "genesis," working through what she conceived of as a change from matriarchy to patriarchy, and ending with "[Virginia] Woolf and [Georgia] O'Keeffe and the first steps in reestablishing the feminine through imagery." The women would be represented with sexually symbolic "butterfly images that are hard, strong, soft, passive, opaque, [and] transparent," which would "all have vaginas so they'll be female butterflies and at the same time be shells, flowers, flesh, forest." All would be "contained within domesticity [on plates], served, and ready to be consumed." The plates, however, would not lie flat on the table. They would rise from the table, "rising up so to speak, from their confinement, but not off the table yet." Chicago had tremendous ambitions for *The Dinner Party* and recorded in her diary her desire to create a "masterpiece."[55]

Chicago worked on *The Dinner Party* in isolation for more than a year, painting and firing test plates and researching women's history to compile a lineage of courageous women stretching from prehistory through the present. She bought a sewing machine capable of embroidery stitching, with the idea of using it to sew a circle of biographical text around each plate on a tablecloth running the length of the table. She settled on an open, equilateral triangular format for the table, with thirteen place settings on each side. The

"How do you identify

an artist? What does an artist look like? When I grew up an artist was defined by a Rembrandt self-portrait. There would be his smock and his beret, velvet usually, and his palette in one hand, his brushes in the other, and these were the symbols of the outward appearance of an artist. So then I say to myself, but I'm a woman, how do I fit into that? Not only that, but I'm a middle-class woman. Not only that, but I'm a Jewish woman. Not only that, I'm not particularly beautiful. In fact, you probably wouldn't pick me out of a crowd. So how would I identify myself as an artist?"

—Miriam Schapiro

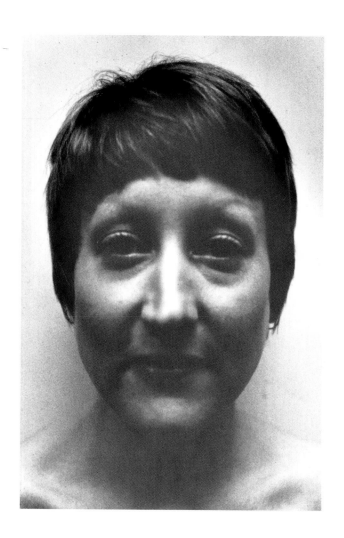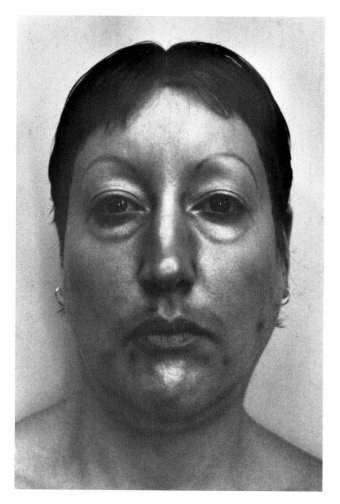

FIG. 55
Martha Wilson. *I Make Up the Image of My Perfection / I Make Up the Image of My Deformity*, 1974 (cat. no. 35).

FIG. 57

Lynn Hershman. *Roberta Breitmore's Construction Chart,* 1973 (cat. no. 33).

FIG. 63
Judy Chicago. *The Dinner Party*, 1979 (cat. no. 1), with the Virginia Woolf and Georgia O'Keeffe place settings in the foreground.

FIG. 64
Karen LeCocq. *Feather Cunt*,
1971 (cat. no. 5).

ular political context of the 1980s—ultimately fore-closes the potential political effects of feminist art-works that are more accessible and enjoyable to a wider spectrum of viewers.[36]

Lippard has insightfully noted that the art world's negative responses to the populism of *The Dinner Party* had everything to do with its specifici-ty of content, its explicit presentation of the kind of allusive ("literary" and "wholly interpretable") ima-gery that is anathema to the ideology of the avant-garde (evident in both Kramer's rejection of the piece for its "vulgar" accessibility and Pollock's dis-missal of feminist art that is "realist in an uncritical

FIG. 65

Judy Chicago posing with her painting *Compressed Women Who Yearned to Be Butterflies*, 1975. This image appeared in her exhibition *Metamorphosis* in Min-neapolis and on the cover of a brochure for the Feminist Art Workshop at the College of Saint Catherine, Saint Paul, in 1975.

way").[37] What has made the debate even more highly charged is that the "wholly interpretable im-agery" of *The Dinner Party*—that is, that aspect of the piece most frequently mentioned in discussions of its success or failure as an artwork—is clearly iden-tifiable as a symbolic representation of a part of the body that is conventionally veiled: the female sex.

Criticism of *The Dinner Party* has often focused on the plates, the majority of which are constructed out of labial folds of clay and decorated with painted vul-var patterns (see fig. 63). This is certainly due at least in part to their transgression of the prohibi-tion against such direct representation. The iconography of the plates developed out of Chicago's extended experimentation with cen-tralized imagery in her work from the late 1960s onward and her interest in using "butterfly," "flower," or "cunt" forms as meta-phors for women's experience.[39] Kra-mer and Hughes thus reviled *The Dinner Party* not only because of its threat to the modernist system of determining aesthetic value but also because of, in Hughes's words, its "relentless concentration on the pu-denda," which clearly threatens the (male) modernist critic's belief in the propriety of the phallus as the proper symbol of creative impulse.

The use of what Kramer called "vulviform image[s]" on the plates al-so threatened the Western aesthetic conventions that privilege images of the female body as fetishistic objects for male spectatorial pleasure but pro-hibit direct representation of the female genitalia. As I have noted else-where, by overtly representing the female sex, the artist endangers the system of aesthetic judgment, since the clearly "obscene" female body is that which must remain outside the realm of high art (since the obscene is that against which high art confirms its purity).[40] Chicago's "relentless" sym-bolization of the female sex threatens the mas-culinist modernist critic's claims of "disinterest-edness." The fact that right-wing members of the United States Congress, debating the proposed gift of *The Dinner Party* to the federally supported University of the District of Columbia in 1991, hysterically denounced the piece for its obscenity

"What is Female Imagery?" Feminist Responses to The Dinner Party and the Politics of "Cunt Art" [38]

FIG. 66

Zippy comic strip created by Bill Griffith in response to the congressional debate over the proposed gift of *The Dinner Party* to the University of the District of Columbia; published in *Arizona Republic* (October 29, 1990).

only confirms this (see figs. 66–67). Notably, Robert K. Dornan derided the piece as "ceramic 3-D pornography," and Dana Rohrbacher called it "weird sexual art" (both are Republicans from California).[41] The convergence of these politicians' reactions with that of Kramer suggests that, in fact, the piece has some very empowering feminist effects in challenging the modernist, masculinist boundaries between art and pornography.

Ironically, however, feminist criticism of *The Dinner Party* has also tended to focus on the plates, with their vulvar, or "cunt," imagery.[42] It was through its deployment of this imagery that *The Dinner Party* came to be seen by many feminists as paradigmatic of all that was problematic about certain strands of 1970s feminism. Although East Coast artists such as Hannah Wilke explored cunt imagery in the 1960s, historically it has been associated with Los Angeles–based feminism—and especially with the writings of Chicago, Arlene Raven, Miriam Schapiro, and Lucy Lippard (then from New York but sympathetic to the Los Angeles feminist art scene).[43] The use of centralized "female" imagery was, from the beginning, challenged by other feminists. Thus, New York critic Cindy Nemser, in an essay published in *The*

FIG. 67

Cover of *Heresies*, no. 14 (May 1978), showing Nancy Reagan fondling the Hypatia plate from *The Dinner Party*.

Feminist Art Journal in 1973–74, described Chicago as the originator of a notion of "cunt art," which "made a case for an intrinsic female imagery created out of round, pulsating, 'womb-like' forms. This 'inner space' ideology," she concludes, "reduces the work of women artists to a simplistic biological formula."[44] Feminist sympathizer Lawrence Alloway, writing in *Art in America* in 1976, stated reductively that in their important 1973 essay "Female Imagery" (see fig. 70), Chicago and Schapiro "claim the central image as an inherent quality, derived from the body image, and consequently different from men's imagery. They relate it to the rediscovery of female sexuality." He dismissed their theory as a "strenuously imposed ideological program."[45]

It is important to distinguish between Chicago's use of centralized imagery in her own work and her notion that a "hidden content" could be found in the work of other women artists, many of whom predated feminism or were antagonistic to it.[46] It was this "hidden content" theory that caused the most consternation among feminist critics, since it seemed to imply that women were biologically driven to produce imagery that mimicked the structure of their own sexual anatomy.

Around 1970 Chicago, motivated by her own

In trying to "peel back" the structure I have used in my work because I felt that I had to "hide" the real content, I found myself making a
vaginal form. I was not so interested in drawing a cunt but there is a big gap between my feelings as a woman and the visual language of the
male culture. Whenever I want to deal with the issue of vulnerability, emotional exposure, or primitive feelings, the only image I can think of is a
vagina, probably because those aspects of the human experience have been relegated to the sphere of the "feminine" and then depreciated. My struggle
has been and is to find a way to let the female experience be represented in such a way that it can stand for those areas of human experience that
male society denies, thus challenging the prevailing values. I don't know how to do that yet. Neither does anyone else. It is the major problem those of us
face who are trying to forge a new language, one that is relevant to women's experience. Recently, I was criticized for the gap that exists between my
"rhetoric", and my work. On one level, the criticism was justified and helped me begin to "peel back" the structure that I had imposed upon my
real content in order to make an identity as an artist in the world. But, in another way, the criticism makes me angry because it implies that
it is my failure as an artist that creates the gap, and that is simply not true. Whatever gap exists grows out of the fact that I have been
trying to bridge a gap that exists in the world— the gap between feminist consciousness and sophisticated art language. In the years I was
developing as an artist, I was consistently rejected as a woman and even more violently rejected if my womanliness was reflected in
my art. Does anyone really understand what it means to have to suppress your femaleness in order to be able to express your artistness—
or what it does to you? I was not willing to be an artist in a closet and now I am not willing to be a woman in a closet. I've chosen
to take on the struggle to be myself in the face of society's rejection in the hope that by so doing, my work will help change society. So now
I'm put down because I haven't got it all together. Even my husband, who loves me and understands my work and my struggle, rejected the image
of my hidden femaleness in this drawing. How many people in this world can stand up to the consistent rejection male culture subjects women to?
How many husbands are willing to struggle with their feelings like my husband did, in order to embrace this drawing? How many women are willing to
face rejection and rejection and rejection and rejection and rejection and rejection and rejection and still insist on exposing their femaleness?

Female Rejection Drawing   Judy Chicago 1974

FIG. 68
Judy Chicago. *Female Rejection Drawing*, from the Rejection Quintet, 1974 (cat. no. 65).

developing identity as a woman artist, not only began producing overtly centralized imagery, often overlaid with explicitly feminist texts, but also began to recognize her own earlier works as subconsciously "female-oriented": "I began to realize," she wrote in her autobiography, "that my real sexual identity had been denied by my culture, and this somehow represented the entire sense of denial I had been experiencing as a woman artist. I felt that if I could symbolize my true sexual nature, I could open up the issue of the nature of my identity as a woman through that symbolic statement." Looking back at her 1968 Dome pieces (see fig. 37, cat. no. 4), small acrylic mounds spray-painted with glowing layers of colored lacquer, Chicago described them as evidence of the return of "female body references . . . reminiscent of the Venus of Willendorf and other early goddesses."[47]

Chicago's Atmospheres, environmental pieces begun in 1969 and continued into the early 1970s, oscillated between abstracted conceptual explorations of the interrelationship of "flesh and landscape" and specifically feminist interventions into the environment through the inclusion of goddess figures.[48] She introduced women performers into the Atmospheres (see fig. 69) as signs of female power, to actualize her desire for the pieces "to transform and soften (i.e. feminize) the environment."[49] Her interest in the goddess, which she shared with feminist artists such as Faith Wilding, Mary Beth Edelson, and Carolee Schneemann, extensively informed *The Dinner Party*—not only in its inclusion of a number of goddess place settings but also in its overall revisionist impulse toward history. Chicago's belief in a prepatriarchal, utopian matriarchal culture, explicitly outlined in the first *Dinner Party* book and concretized in the idealizing, abstract representations of the goddess plates and runners, has been criticized as naive.[50] But the *idea* of the mythical goddess was clearly powerfully enabling for these artists, serving as a site of projection that allowed them to actualize their own attempts to attain the kind of transcendence conventionally reserved for men (the "central core" image played the same empowering role).[51]

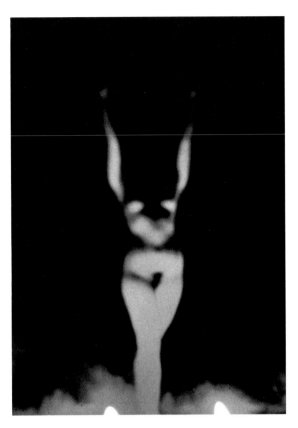

FIG. 69
Judy Chicago. *Goddess*, 1970, from the Atmospheres; performance in Fresno, California.

By 1973 Chicago had fully established in two and three dimensions this centralized imagery—radiating, pulsating rings and folds of brilliantly colored, airbrushed paint—which she would develop into the sculptural vulvar forms of the *Dinner Party* plates. Whereas her Domes "subconsciously" suggested the rounded, centralized forms of the breasts or womb, Chicago's pictorial forays into the "central core" are much more literal. In *Female Rejection Drawing* (fig. 68, cat. no. 65), also known as *Peeling Back*, a particularly dramatic and evocative image from the Rejection Quintet of 1974, she combined the formal structure of the central core, here a delicately colored series of labial folds emerging from a painfully torn containing surface, with an extensive handwritten text describing her feelings of exposure, fear, and anguish at being judged and rejected by the male-dominated art world.[52]

Female Rejection Drawing, one of Chicago's most explicitly autobiographical images, seems to sum up in vibrant, material terms both her commitment to the notion of a centralized form as a means of reclaiming the female body from patriarchy in an empowering way and her insistence, common in the women's movement in general at this time, on the importance of expressing personal issues in political terms. A central component of Chicago's coming to consciousness as a feminist artist in the 1970s was her desire to "peel back" the repressed content of her work, to "put together the sophisticated formal language of contemporary art with the rather raw and unexpressed subject matter I wanted to begin to deal with. . . . I peeled back my coded imagery and finally broke through to the beginning of new imagery and the reappearance of the butterfly. . . . This became pivotal in the imagery of *The Dinner Party*."[53] *Female Rejection Drawing* exemplifies Chicago's desire to transform the female sex from a locus of objectification to a powerful sign of *subjectivity* through imagery that visualized the "orgiastic throbbing [and] . . . highly focussed feeling of clitoral sensation" that signaled women as desiring subjects rather than mere objects of desire.[54]

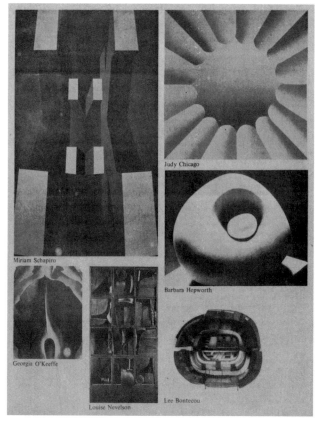

FIG. 70

Page from Judy Chicago and Miriam Schapiro's "Female Imagery," published in *Womanspace Journal* 1 (Summer 1973), showing women's artworks with centralized imagery.

Chicago's theory of the central-core image as the reflection of a "female sensibility" became more problematic when she extended this formal symbology to the work of other artists. In "Female Imagery" Chicago and Schapiro solidified this theory, asking: "What does it feel like to be a woman? To be formed around a central core and have a secret place which can be entered and which is also a passageway from which life emerges?" They conclude by suggesting that "women artists have used the central cavity which defines them as women as the framework for an imagery which allows for the complete reversal of the way in which women are seen by the culture. That is, to be a woman is to be an object of contempt and the vagina, stamp of femaleness, is devalued. The woman artists [*sic*], seeing herself as loathed, takes that very mark of her otherness and by asserting it as the hallmark of her iconography, establishes a vehicle by which to state the truth and beauty of her identity."[55]

In the early essays on this subject, a hesitancy in defining the sources of this "female sensibility" is apparent. While they saw the crucial political importance of defining a particular female approach to artistic form, feminists such as Chicago and Schapiro were loath to fix this form, its sources or meanings, in any determinate way.[56] Thus, they explicitly state that "the visual symbology we have been describing must not be seen in a simplistic sense as 'vaginal or womb art'" and stress that it is the "way in which women are seen by the culture" that is at issue. Likewise, Raven insisted in 1975 that the "female experience . . . is socially defined and cultural rather than biological, innate, or personal."[57] In an earlier essay she also underlined the importance of the feminist insistence on *content* (that is, the representation or evocation of "female experience") as an attack on modernist formalism and the capitalist structure it serves.[58] She questioned the "very word *feminine*," which, she argued, "refers to the characteristics of a biological female . . . [and] is a fluid term which is effected [*sic*] by the historical moment to which it is applied. 'Feminine' characteristics change according to the political,

FIG. 82
Sandra Orgel. *Ironing*, 1972 (cat. no. 45).

Identifying with Judy Chicago

critics of *The Dinner Party* who consider her impulse to connect with the totality of humanity a fantasy, not an accomplishable feat, and who are attentive to the ways in which her belief in the universality of her artwork allies her with existing systems of power. According to the alternative logic these critics unfold, the nuns would have understood Chicago because both she and they claim to transcend the limitations of the world around them, in a way that weds her and them to authority as it is already configured.

One early and eloquent challenge to Judy Chicago's sense of her work's universal appeal was posed by Alice Walker. Writing in 1979 in *Ms.* magazine, Walker expressed her concern that Chicago's *Dinner Party*, like other contemporary attempts by white women to revise cultural history along feminist lines, revealed no awareness of the complexity and specificity of black women's life situations. She questions why the only *Dinner Party* plate explicitly dedicated to a black woman—the Sojourner Truth plate (fig. 88)—shows a semi-illusionistic set of weeping, struggling faces instead of the abstracted vulvar butterfly common to the majority of the

FIG. 88
Judy Chicago. *Sojourner Truth Plate,* from *The Dinner Party,* 1979 (cat. no. 1); china paint on porcelain; diam: 14 in.

FIG. 89
Judy Chicago. *Tapestry Banners,* from *The Dinner Party,* 1979 (cat. no. 1).

other thirty-eight plates. This special treatment, she argues, depletes Sojourner Truth's history as well as that of every black woman obliged to look to this single image for recognition of her unique and particular heritage and lived experiences: "To think of black women is impossible if you cannot imagine them with vaginas. Sojourner Truth certainly had a vagina, as note her lament about her children, born of her body and sold into slavery. Note her comment . . . that when she cried out with a mother's grief, none but Jesus heard her. Surely a vagina has to be acknowledged when one reads these words. (A vagina the color of raspberries and blackberries—or scuppernongs and muscadines—and of that strong, silvery sweetness, with, as well, a sharp flavor of salt.)" [5]

As I look closely at *The Dinner Party* through the lens this analysis provides, the work shows an increasingly familiar face. Walker helps locate its universalism within a sphere of blind whiteness—an invented, sheltering place where thoughts and questions and worries about racial tensions and specificities do not soak and burn daily in the pores but instead are regarded as luxuries or irritants or grounds for self-congratulation. I know it well; I

was born into this blind white place. My great-grandparents carved it out for me at the turn of this century, and many of us in succeeding generations have padded it with plusher, more opaque linings.

Like Chicago's first-generation Jewish-American forbears, my great-grandparents did not have the mythical stuff of whiteness with them when they came over from Eastern Europe. Nor was it simply handed to them when they landed. In the Old Country they had experienced the Jew-Gentile split as a primary division in their lives, a division traceable in the lines of state law and community custom that kept them cordoned into shtetels, little ghetto towns marked off from European culture's mainstream. As David Roediger has noted, the questions of whether and to what extent pre-twentieth-century Europeans of any ethnic or religious cast understood Jewishness as a racial identity have yet to be satisfactorily addressed. [6]

What is certain is that, upon their entry into America, my ancestors would have been confronted by an official, enforced racial division between a valued whiteness and a devalued blackness.

FIG. 97
Yoko Ono. *Cut Piece*, 1964 (cat. no. 61).

FIG. 98
Sue Williams. *A Funny Thing Happened*, 1992 (cat. no. 69).

Howardena Pindell. *Autobiography: Earth/Eyes/Injuries,* 1987 (cat. no. 67).

Rereading the
Readings of
The Dinner Party
in Europe

Anette Kubitza

When *The Dinner Party* (fig. 8, cat. no. 1) was first exhibited, in 1979, one reviewer mused: "Years from now it will be interesting to see if [*The Dinner Party*] is regarded as a landmark in the recognition of women, an outdated monument or a temple in honor of [Judy] Chicago."[2] Looking back a decade and a half later, it is apparent that the answer to the question depends on who is asked, on who is reading the artwork. The reception of *The Dinner Party*, more than that of any work of art conceived under the banner of the women's movement, shows that feminism and feminist art are volatile concepts. The European reception of the piece in particular reveals that an artwork labeled feminist by its maker will not necessarily be *read* as a feminist work of art.

After its first showing, *The Dinner Party* traveled for nearly a decade through the United States, Canada, Great Britain, Germany, and Australia. In Europe the reception of the piece followed the peculiar pattern established in the United States and Canada; the harsh criticism of the mainstream press stood in sharp contrast to the euphoric praise of the tens of thousands of women who organized, supported, and visited the shows. In Europe, as in North America, the piece was promoted by countless individual women and grassroots women's organizations, who faced resistance from the art establishment. Thus, *The Dinner Party* became more than just another work of art, and the exhibitions of the piece became events of the women's movement.

Feminists have not, however, been unanimous in their support of *The Dinner Party*. They have reviewed it critically since it was first exhibited. When the piece reached Europe in 1984, ten years after its initial conception, it met with outright rejection and bitter accusations from within the ranks of feminists. While some British and

The other instance is the 1980 multiprojector slide show *In the Beginning of the End*, by Danish artist Maj Skadegaard and German artist Renate Stendahl.[21] This audiovisual work, which tells the story of the ousting of matriarchal cultures and the systematic oppression of women under patriarchy, includes slides of *The Dinner Party* along with images of works by other twentieth-century women artists such as Mary Beth Edelson, Frida Kahlo, and Ana Mendieta. In Skadegaard and Stendahl's show *The Dinner Party* functions as a feminist vision of a better future for women, based on an appreciation of matriarchal cultures.

In Europe, as in the United States and Canada, most people who expressed appreciation for *The Dinner Party* were not involved in the art world. They were attracted for many reasons: the piece's documentary value, its enlightening imagery, its splendor, its crafts, and its spirituality. And in Europe, as in the United States, exhibitions of the piece took place largely without the support of the art world. Although women from several European countries showed interest in the piece, only in Great Britain and Germany was there sufficient commitment by private organizations to carry through an exhibition.[22] I will focus here on *The Dinner Party*'s reception in those two countries.

Great Britain: Idiosyncrasies of Feminist Cultural Discourse

In 1984 *The Dinner Party* left the North American continent to travel to Edinburgh and then, in 1985, to London. The work came to Great Britain at the invitation of Diane Robson, who had formed the one-woman organization Diehard Productions to raise funds and to find a site for its exhibition. She organized the first show as part of the Edinburgh Fringe Festival, which, as an alternative to the huge international Edinburgh summer festival, hosts art, theater, and music events in nontraditional spaces. In Edinburgh Robson had a former church, Victoria Hall, renovated as an exhibition space for *The Dinner Party*; in London she rented a converted warehouse for its display.

While Robson continued the pattern of exceptional personal commitment which had been established in the United States to enable the showing of *The Dinner Party*, she did not enjoy the same success as her American sisters when it came to fundraising. This can be explained by the absence of the kind of grassroots support from women that had helped ensure *The Dinner Party*'s success elsewhere. Robson, who came to the project with a background in theater production, did not reach out and build up this kind of support. Even though her exhibitions were a financial fiasco, however, they were extraordinarily well attended. Despite negative reviews,[23] the two-month presentation in London alone attracted more than forty thousand people. In Britain, as in the United States and Canada, the visitors to the shows were mostly women interested in the needlework and china-painting techniques or in the piece's feminist message; they were not, by and large, familiar with art world politics and art historical issues.[24] While the attendance numbers suggest a hunger for the kinds of knowledge and identification promised by *The Dinner Party*, British feminist art theory and practice, which at the time were heavily influenced by psychoanalysis and poststructuralism, were not sympathetic to approaches suited to the needs of a broader audience.

Although the development of the British women artists' movement in the late 1960s and early 1970s closely paralleled that of its American counterpart, the politics of the movement came to center around socialist politics rather than a politics of difference that celebrated a separate culture of women and positively emphasized women's difference from men. A materialist approach to the sexual division of labor, informed by Marxist theory, dominated feminist art practice in Britain in the 1970s. For example, in 1975 artists Margaret Harrison, Kay Hunt, and Mary Kelly, interested in Britain's workers' culture and its unionist tradition, collaborated in staging an exhibition called *Women and Work*. This documentary show on women workers in the Southwark Metal Box Company factory combined filmic material with enlargements of charts and tables comparing women and men at work. The show was an attempt to analyze how the traditional sexual division of labor and ideals of femininity play into the processes of industrial production and have

Judy Chicago; embroidered by **Jane Gaddie Thompson**. *Birth Tear E-2*, 1982, from *The Birth Project*, 1980–85 (cat. no. 27).

Toward the end of the 1970s women in Germany increasingly embraced an ideology of gender difference, influenced by feminist cultural ideas and feminist spiritualism from the United States, as well as by the philosophical and literary texts of new French feminism, notably Luce Irigaray's writings. These German feminists rejected what they perceived as "male" ways of thinking and behaving and instead favored a woman-centered perspective that reevaluated women's reproductive functions, exploring traditional "female" values such as pacifism and a gentler approach to nature and the earth. The feminist emphasis on those values made women special advocates of the peace and environmental movements, assigning them the role of bringing about a better future.

But in the wake of the reactionary, antifeminist politics of the conservative German government elected in 1982, this position was discredited by some factions of the women's movement for its supposed compatibility with patriarchal policies. Its reliance on gender stereotypes at a time when dominant culture stressed conventional signs of gender difference was considered dangerous. Already in 1983 Alice Schwarzer, editor of *Emma* (Germany's most widely read feminist magazine), tempered her triumphant announcement of the demise of gynocentrism with a warning: "The worst phases of the biological argument—from the myth of nature to the new ideology of motherhood—have been transcended. Women are becoming more aggressive; many have seen that we cannot defend the rights we painfully fought for with the help of the Moon Goddess. But especially in these times of mass unemployment and the imperious propagation of 'family values' and the 'female role,' the fear of a regression to the new/old feminine mystique is unfortunately as alive as ever."[56]

Despite Schwarzer's call for an end to gynocentrism, a new wave of gynocentric feminist ideas coincided with the exhibition of *The Dinner Party* in Germany. In March 1987, only a couple of months before the opening, a group of women (many of them members of the left-wing Green party) surprised the press and their female colleagues in Bonn with what came to be known as the *Müttermanifest* (Manifesto of mothers). They demanded the restructuring of society as well as party politics with regard to the needs of mothers.[57] The manifesto, which was based on the results of a conference of mothers and their supporters in 1986, triggered a wave of criticism. Some female Green party members considered it a call for a return to traditional gender roles and dismissed its proponents as frustrated young academics who had become trapped in the maternal role because of a lack of employment opportunities.[58]

The reception of *The Dinner Party* in Germany mirrors these debates. While a group of women who embraced gynocentric feminist politics and spiritual feminism celebrated the work as the cultural centerpiece of their movement, others, mostly feminist scholars belonging to the socialist wing, considered Chicago an essentialist bent on propagating stereotypical ideologies of motherhood and dismissed her work as a threat to the goals of feminism. For both groups *The Dinner Party* became a convenient vehicle for airing their feminist beliefs in the broader public sphere. The programmatic silence of male critics, and the lack of a tightly knit feminist art movement that would provide a professional context, allowed the turmoil around the piece to escalate into a *Weiberkrach* ("cat fight"), moving beyond a debate about the "correct" understanding of *The Dinner Party* to a conflict over the meaning of feminism itself.

At times allegations were made quite randomly and had little to do with the work itself, as a retrospective evaluation by Gisela Brackert, head of women's programming for a state radio station, suggests: "Anything that ever bothered anyone about the so-called zeitgeist—postmodernism, the women's movement, the new ideology of motherhood, the turn toward neoconservatism—it could be found in *The Dinner Party*, which was created in California a decade ago."[59]

When knowledge about the artwork first spread to Germany in the early 1980s, it coincided with a newly evolving interest in the study of women's history and cultural achievements. But it also fit into the agenda of those feminists whose approach had been prematurely pronounced dead by

Schwarzer: spiritual and gynocentric feminists who linked their struggle for a better future to a matriarchal past. In 1982 Heide Göttner-Abendroth, a well-known scholar of matriarchy, discussed *The Dinner Party* at length in her book on the principles of a matriarchal aesthetic, thereby influencing the early appraisal of the work in Germany.[60] The broadcast of an edited version of Johanna Demetrakas's 1980 documentary *Right out of History: The Making of Judy Chicago's "The Dinner Party"* on German television in 1983 and 1984, the discussion of *The Dinner Party* on several radio programs, and the publication of Chicago's autobiography in German helped spark the interest of a broader audience.[61]

The Dinner Party was pushed to the forefront of women's cultural politics in the mid-1980s by the commitment of Dagmar von Garnier and Anne-Marie Gesse, two Frankfurt women who founded the organization Die Dinner Party in Deutschland (The Dinner Party in Germany) with the goal of "creating so much publicity that this artwork—in spite of the substantial resistance of the established art world—will be exhibited."[62] In contrast to Diane Robson in Britain, von Garnier and Gesse were able to mobilize substantial support before inviting *The Dinner Party* to Germany. What started as a small initiative soon became a vast network of primarily female supporters from Germany, Austria, and Switzerland. Members of the core group, led by von Garnier, translated and tried (unsuccessfully) to publish Chicago's two volumes on *The Dinner Party*, held numerous talks, and distributed materials about the piece, including seven newsletters written by von Garnier between June 1985 and July 1986, which were mailed to interested groups and individuals.

The organization's primary focus was on finding a suitable exhibition space. Recognizing the historical and ideological importance of placing women's art in a state-run art institution and mindful of the financial problems encountered in Great Britain, the organization decided to solicit the commitment of art world officials.[63] The cities of Offenbach and Wiesbaden expressed great interest in exhibiting *The Dinner Party*—the mayor of the latter proposed to erect a huge tent on the city common for this purpose—but Frankfurt, one of the largest German cities, was favored by the organizers

because of its central location and the fact that it was home to many of the group's members.[64] Cultural officials there, however, were initially not supportive: Hilmar Hoffmann, head of the city's cultural affairs department, proffered technical reasons for not showing *The Dinner Party*, and Christoph Vitali, director of the newly opened Schirn Kunsthalle, openly expressed reservations regarding the work's artistic merits.[65] Despite these negative responses, however, *The Dinner Party* entered local politics via a petition submitted by the Social Democratic Party to the city's cultural affairs committee. A member of that committee defended the petition, stating: "For an artwork that has attracted interest worldwide, one ought to find a space in Frankfurt as well."[66] A year later, in the spring of 1987, *The Dinner Party* was exhibited at the Schirn Kunsthalle. Vitali explained his turnabout by citing the commitment of a large number of women to the piece, which had positively influenced art world officials.[67]

Decisive for this change of mind was a huge gala, known as the Banquet of a Thousand Women, which was hosted in Frankfurt by von Garnier and her organization in the summer of 1986. This gala, a highly controversial event in its own right, was an outstanding event in *The Dinner Party*'s reception in Germany and had a powerful influence on how the piece was perceived when it arrived there the following year. Women from all over Europe were invited to participate in the gala, with the admission fee of 390 marks (about $240) per person going to support further activities promoting the showing of *The Dinner Party* in Germany. Each participant was asked to represent one of the 1,038 figures whose names appear in the piece, to dress in costume, and to be able to inform other guests about her chosen woman's story. On June 7, 1986, approximately six hundred women clad in elaborate historical and mythical garb gathered at Frankfurt's opera house to celebrate the heritage of women. Many guests had spent months researching the life of the woman they represented and identified strongly with their roles.[68] The stories of the historical and mythical figures in *The Dinner Party* reduce Chicago's sexual imagery to a symbol of essential femaleness in the first place. In Germany Chicago's writings have often been interpreted as proposing the use of vulvar imagery as a deterministic symbol of an innate difference between women and men. Quoting Chicago's description of the plate for the primordial goddess, the editors of *FrauenKunstWissenschaft* maintained that her rhetoric supported an interpretation of the imagery in general as symbolic of female fertility and procreative powers, reducing women to these functions.[97] In particular, Chicago's frequent use of the word *femaleness* (in German, translated as *Weiblichkeit*, an ideologically loaded term that also means "femininity") made German critics suspicious and influenced their understanding of her vulvar imagery.[98] At the time *The Dinner Party* was exhibited in Germany, the term *Weiblichkeit* was not popular in feminist discourse, and a woman using it was quickly accused of being essentialist.

A closer look at the work itself, however, reveals that, although Chicago offers the women represented in *The Dinner Party* as role models, she does not celebrate a traditional female identity. Her selection of mythological and historical figures instead suggests that these women are offered as role models precisely because they had transcended a traditional female role; their potential had not been exhausted in fulfilling reproductive functions. In fact, a more pointed criticism of Chicago's approach might be that she does not question the traditional male ideal of public success but, rather, attempts to legitimate women within this ideal.

An explanation for the prevalence of this kind of reductive reading of *The Dinner Party*'s vulvar imagery among German scholars can be found in the dominant feminist discourse of that time as well as in the specific circumstances of the Frankfurt exhibition. The debate surrounding the *Müttermanifest*, which coincided with the exhibition of *The Dinner Party* in Germany, may well have informed the interpretations of the work as fostering essentialist ideas about women and, in particular, a regressive ideology of motherhood. The controversy surrounding

the gala also clearly paved the way for a reading that focused on women's reproductive powers.[99]

Chicago herself facilitated this interpretation by using the exhibition of *The Dinner Party* in Frankfurt to advertise her more recent work, *The Birth Project* (1980–85; see fig. 103, cat. no. 27). With statements such as "Giving birth is common to all women. That is their essential difference from men,"[100] she risked limiting the meaning of her earlier work. Not surprisingly, German reviewers saw *The Dinner Party*'s message as closely linked to that of *The Birth Project*, some calling the latter a logical continuation of the former.[101] One of the reviews featured a photomontage of Chicago and Pope John Paul II sitting harmoniously at the dinner table, chatting about Chicago's *Birth Project*.[102] This work, which metaphorically explores the birth experience, was apparently seen by German feminist critics as having an implicitly anti–abortion-rights agenda and supporting a traditional view of motherhood.

Chicago's approach to motherhood contrasts with that of German feminist artist Annegret Soltau. In her 1980–82 installation *Schwanger Sein* (Being pregnant; fig. 108), Soltau broke radically with clichés of idealized motherhood, addressing birth and motherhood on the level of concrete experiences and emotions. She investigated her feelings of ambivalence as she faced the dilemma of simultaneously fulfilling the roles of artist and mother, with the conflicting expectations attached to each. In one sequence a scythe is lowered dangerously close to her supine pregnant body, symbolizing the existential threat the artist perceived in becoming a mother, a nurturer of another life.[103] Although Soltau was criticized by the art establishment and by her female colleagues for dealing with this topic at all, her iconoclastic and critical approach to women's roles was in tune with dominant feminist ideas of the 1980s in Germany.

Despite the criticisms of some German feminists, *The Dinner Party* did not completely lose its impact as an enlightening feminist monument. Statements by women linked to the organization Das Erbe der Frauen, who unofficially guided groups through the Frankfurt exhibition, support Joani Blank's observation that many women have yet to be exposed to depictions of female genitals as an important source of self-knowledge.[104] The

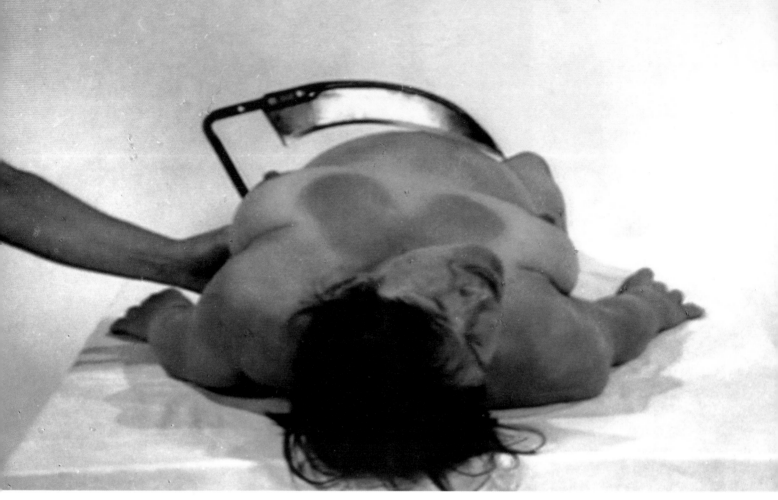

FIG. 108
Annegret Soltau (b. Lüneburg, Germany, 1946). *Schwanger Sein* (Being pregnant), 1980–82; still photograph from video installation. Courtesy of the artist.

exhibition guides noted that the women in their groups, especially older women who had not taken part in the sexual revolution of the 1960s, were shocked and overwhelmed by the overt, if sanitized, depiction of female genitals in *The Dinner Party*.[105] One guide thought that each visitor's reaction to the vulvar imagery reflected her relationship to her own sexual organ, which was either "schön oder Scham" (beautiful or shameful/pubic). Another argued that the delayed development of the women's movement in Germany, at least in relation to the United States, was responsible for these strong reactions. The exhibition also became a locus for raising political issues (for example, the Sojourner Truth plate provided an occasion to talk about the practice of clitoridectomy), as well as general issues of the representation of women in patriarchal society.

"Beware of Fascist Feminism"

The advent of the women's movement brought forth certain expectations of woman artists. As German filmmaker Helke Sander has argued, since the rise of the women's movement, female artists

have been confronted with claims by a diverse group of people with an unusually high desire for self-reflection and identification, a desire to find their ideas and experiences expressed.[106] Although it is true that the parameters for the reception of works of art labeled feminist are set by the individual viewer's expectations, those expectations are in turn shaped within specific contexts, which are decisive in informing the ways in which viewers evaluate and phrase their encounters.

An examination of *The Dinner Party*'s reception in Great Britain and Germany shows that reactions to the piece have differed greatly among women, according to both their individual needs and their stance within feminist politics. While one clearly cannot generalize about reactions to the piece in these countries, some general observations can be made about the contexts in which these encounters took place. In both countries dominant feminist ideas of the 1980s, which were informed by poststructuralism, Marxist theory, and an aversion to gynocentrism, helped shape a critical stance toward the work.

Beyond the politics of feminism some cultural differences surfaced in the debate over the American-made piece. British feminist artists and art theorists, for example, show a much stronger involvement with questions of social and economic class as well as psychoanalytic theory. Their highly theoretical approach contrasts with Chicago's pragmatic, celebratory strategy, which they saw as sometimes glossing over differences and contradictions. The legacy of Nazism in Germany indirectly influenced interpretations of *The Dinner Party* and the events surrounding its exhibition there. Overreaction to what many regarded as its universalism and essentialism, exacerbated by the somewhat monumentalizing celebration of the work prior to its exhibition in Frankfurt, played a part in preventing a more rational consideration of *The Dinner Party* in Germany.

The Dinner Party cannot be expected to satisfy all of the demands brought to it by its diverse audiences. It is unquestionably a phenomenon of the decade of its making: the search for lost knowledge about women's past, their cultural heritage, their sexuality, and their spirituality was at the forefront of the feminist agenda in the 1970s. But the fact that *The Dinner Party* cannot keep step with rapidly changing feminist politics and ideas, that it is at odds with the expectations of many feminists today, does not necessarily mean that it should lose its status as feminist art.

As New Zealand artist Carole Shepheard, who uses *The Dinner Party* in her teaching, has observed: "There seems to be this need to dismiss critical work done at an earlier time in the women's art movement and to wage a war of 'born-again' sophistication and theoretical cloaking against such an important and still relevant installation."[107] *The Dinner Party*'s European reception offers a prime example of the tendency of feminist art critics during the 1980s to distance themselves from the artists who originated and developed the women's art movement in the 1970s. The work of these artists is generally equated with an essentialist and reactionary feminism and considered obsolete.[108]

Again, the questions arise of who defines the feminist cultural field and to whose advantage this definition is made. At times feminist art critics of the 1980s assumed control of the feminist cultural field in a rather totalitarian way. Some German feminist critics in particular phrased their critiques of *The Dinner Party* in a manner that sometimes frighteningly evoked the vocabulary used during the Nazi period to exclude "degenerate" art and art by Jews from the official art world.

Hannah Wilke, on a 1977 poster showing her naked upper body covered with tiny chewing-gum vulvae, warned: "Marxism and Art: Beware of Fascist Feminism" (fig. 109). Mocking her feminist critics, Wilke wanted to draw attention to the dangers of a prescriptive, limiting feminism: "I made [this poster], because I felt feminism could easily become fascistic if people believe that feminism is only their kind of feminism, and not my kind of feminism, or her kind of feminism, or his kind of feminism."[109] Wilke—who often used herself, especially her naked body, in her work—faced strong

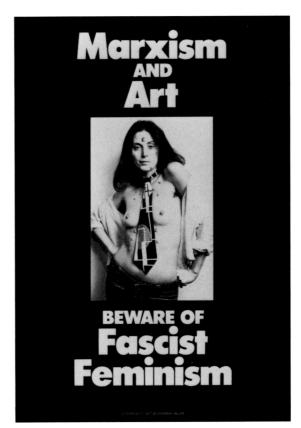

FIG. 109

Hannah Wilke. *Marxism and Art: Beware of Fascist Feminism*, 1977; offset lithograph on heavy paper; 11¼ x 9 in. Courtesy Ronald Feldman Fine Arts, New York.

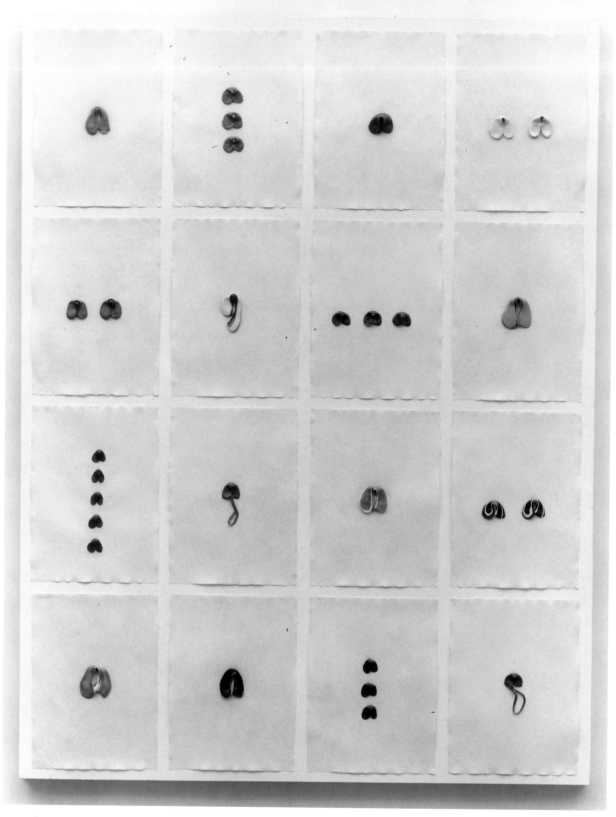

FIG. 110

Hannah Wilke. *Mastication Box Sculpture*, 1975, from *S.O.S. Starification Object Series*, 1974–82 (cat. no. 8).

"The injunction against essentialism seems a continuation of the repression by Western civilization of woman's experience (of which sexuality is only a part), and it should be defied, no matter what the risk."

—Mira Schor

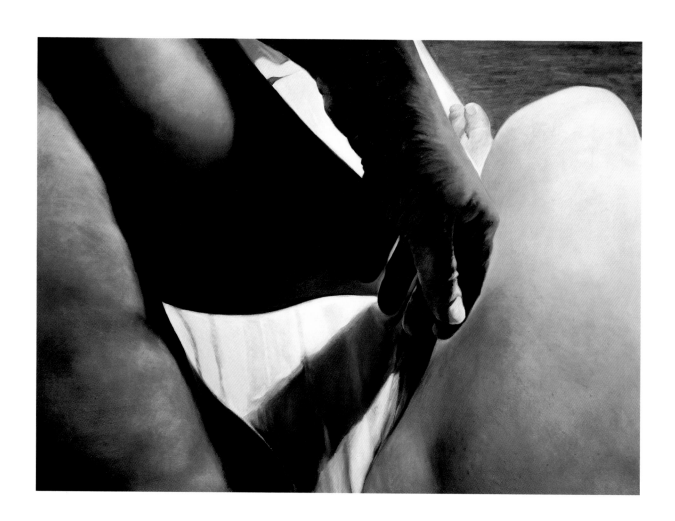

FIG. 113
Joan Semmel. *Hand Down*, 1977 (cat. no. 71).

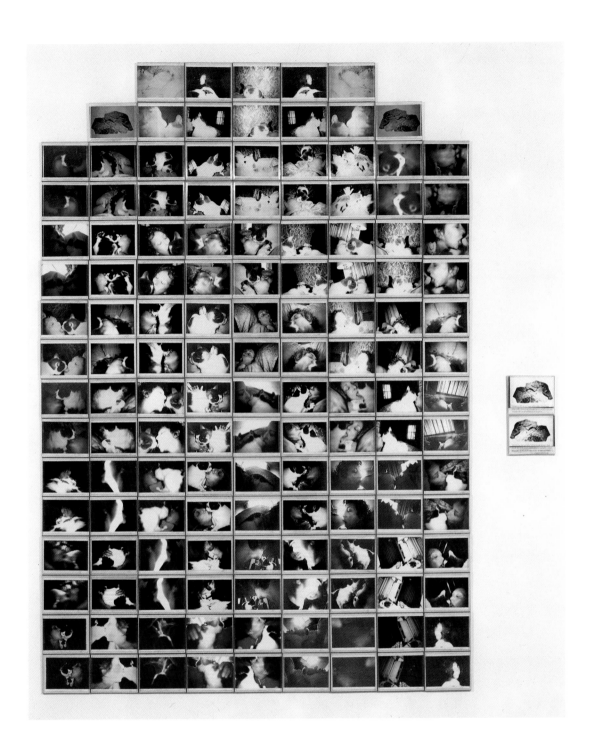

FIG. 114
Carolee Schneemann. *Infinity Kisses*, 1981–87 (cat. no. 73).

FIG. 115

Lorraine O'Grady. *The Clearing; or, Cortez and La Malinche, Thomas Jefferson and Sally Hemings, N. and Me,* 1991 (cat. no. 75).

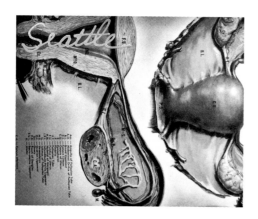

FIGS. 116–17
Annie Sprinkle. *A Public Cervix Announcement* (left, detail), 1992–94; *Temple of the Sacred Prostitute* (right, detail), 1992–94 (cat. nos. 77–78).

FIG. 118
June Wayne. *Jock for Sport*, 1980 (cat. no. 72).

Beneath the Green Veil: The Body in/of New Feminist Art

Susan Kandel

*How does a body figure on its surface the very
invisibility of its hidden depth?*

Judith Butler, *Gender Trouble*

*The true mystery of the world is the visible,
not the invisible.*

Oscar Wilde, *The Picture of Dorian Gray*

First Truths

In *Hard Core*, her genealogy of pornographic film, Linda Williams posits the phantom truth of that genre—the truth that is sought after, though always already unattainable, the truth that engenders the fiction, though never consummated in or by it. This is the truth of female sexual pleasure, the elusive truth of the female body.

It is possible to represent the physical pleasure of the male by showing the mechanics of erection and ejaculation (however counterfeit the arousal). Female sexual pleasure is less accommodating. It operates by stealth: hooded, under cover, between the skin's folds. And so, Williams writes, "the animating male fantasy of hard-core cinema might therefore be described as the (impossible) attempt to capture visually this frenzy of the visible in a female body whose orgasmic excitement can never be objectively measured."[1]

If the pornographic regime is sited in the fold between the visible and the invisible, its reigning figure is the "beaver shot," a close-up view of a woman with her legs apart, her labia spread, and her genitals exposed. Freud refers to the female genitalia as "nothing to see." This "nothing to see," however, is precisely what is to be seen behind pornography's ubiquitous, if metaphorical, green door.[2] There, deep inside a fantasy of nonstop desire, the knowledge that escaped the father of psychoanalysis is envisioned. Yet what secrets are revealed? Perhaps it is merely that another door is cracked open. The vagina is, after all, slippery—a zone where trespass is more than a tease but less than a promise.

Behind the green door a central hole contracts and expands, clicks around in a circle, twists, turns, thrusts forward, and becomes soft, consecutively and simultaneously. These are the words Judy Chicago uses to describe a 1969–70 series of paintings. These paintings transcribe a continuum of feeling, miming "the dissolving sensation that occurs during orgasm." The closed forms Chicago once favored here give way to open forms, which the artist likens to "doughnuts, stars, and revolving mounds."[3] In

FIG. 123

Zoe Leonard (b. Liberty, New York, 1961). Untitled installation at the Neue Galerie, Kassel, Germany, June 13–September 20, 1992. Courtesy Paula Cooper Gallery, New York.

Kassel, as "sensational . . . flabbergasting . . . a gesture of blasphemy . . . furious . . . a rough and tumble lovers' quarrel."[17] Schjeldahl's breathless language—gasped out in the interval between "shock" and "heightened alertness"—seems to betray both excitement and discomfiture, a masculine reaction not incommensurate with the experience of standing in a room consecrated to the vagina.

Chicago's *Menstruation Bathroom* (fig. 125, cat. no. 24), at the center of the Feminist Art Program's 1972 Womanhouse, was also consecrated to the vagina. Yet it was not a room one could stand in. One could only peer into it, according to Chicago, "through a thin veil of gauze, which made the room a sanctum."[18] The *Menstruation Bathroom* was about the look as well as the body. A metaphor wrapped around a fact, it figured the body as house housing the body in the house—or at least the latter's detritus, the damning evidence of its "monstrous" femininity.

In many ways Leonard's maneuver was far more blunt. Into the Neue Galerie's collection of eighteenth-century German portraits of wives, mistresses, and daughters—attired in the most splendid array of silks, laces, bustles, and brocades—she slipped a series of black-and-white photographs of female genitals, a gesture both cunning and blatant (see fig. 123). If every art object is a beaver shot in disguise—something to gape at, to possess, something in and through which a sense of the self is derived—then Leonard is merely stating the obvious. One must, however, always beware the obvious, which too easily insinuates itself into the realm of the visible.

Indeed, Leonard's crotch shots are appropriated from a source that was long invisible: Gustave Courbet's legendary "missing" painting of 1866, *L'origine du monde* (The origin of the world; fig. 126). The painting, said to have disappeared after World War II from a collection in Budapest, resurfaced after the war in France, hung for a time in Jacques

Lacan's country house, and then vanished. It was, until recently, considered "lost" and was known only through a series of more or less accurate black-and-white reproductions.[19] Linda Nochlin described it in 1986 as "a lost original, an original which is itself, in both the literal and the figurative senses of the word, an origin." It is an origin in that it enacts the prototypical art historical scenario: the search for the ultimate meaning of the work of art. As Nochlin points out, "this ultimate-meaning-to-be-penetrated might be considered the 'reality' of woman herself, the truth of the ultimate Other."[20]

L'origine du monde was commissioned in 1866 by Khalil Bey, the Turkish ambassador to Saint Petersburg and a well-known collector of erotica. Maxime Du Camp, the amateur photographer and man of letters, described the painting and its patron in his 1878–79 tome *Les convulsions de Paris* (a memoir of the Commune of 1871):

> To please a Moslem who paid for his whims in gold, and who, for a time, enjoyed a certain notoriety in Paris because of his prodigalities, Courbet . . . painted a portrait of a woman which is difficult to describe. In the dressing room of this foreign personage one sees a

FIG. 124
Christine Lidrbauch. *Untitled Drawing*, 1991 (cat. no. 30).

FIG. 125 (OPPOSITE)
Judy Chicago. *Menstruation Bathroom*, 1972 (re-created 1995) (cat. no. 24).

"Uncovering the lost mysteries and womanhistories of the Matriarchy . . . [we] enrich our present by increasing the threads of continuity with our ancient sisters. To know and understand our foremothers is to give us more insight into our circumstances, enhance our self-image, and provide a firmer ground in which to restore a woman to her rightful place."

—Mary Beth Edelson

FIG. 128

Ana Mendieta. *Untitled*, 1976, from Silueta Works in Iowa, 1976–78 (cat. no. 79).

FIG. 129

Yolanda M. López. *Portrait of the Artist as the Virgin of Guadalupe,* 1978 (cat. no. 82).

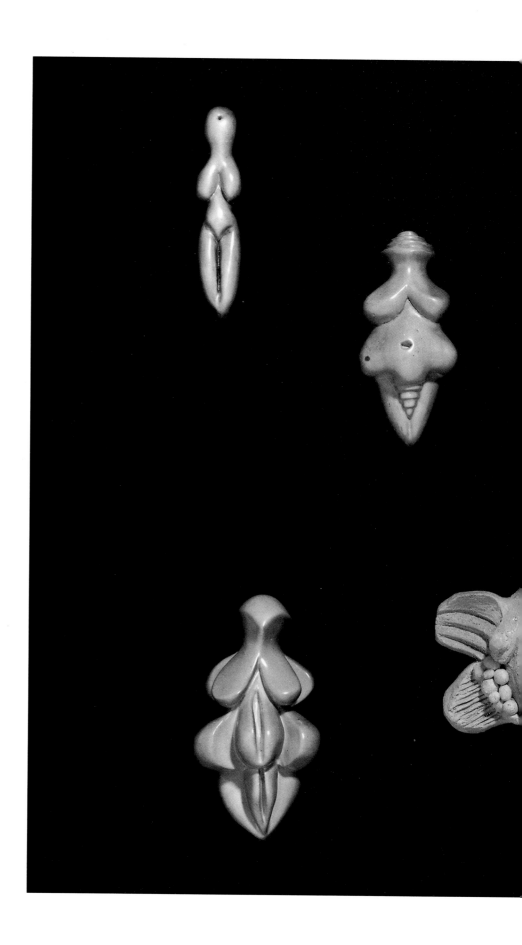

FIG. 130
Judy Chicago. *Untitled*, from the Goddess Figures Series, 1977 (cat. no. 81).

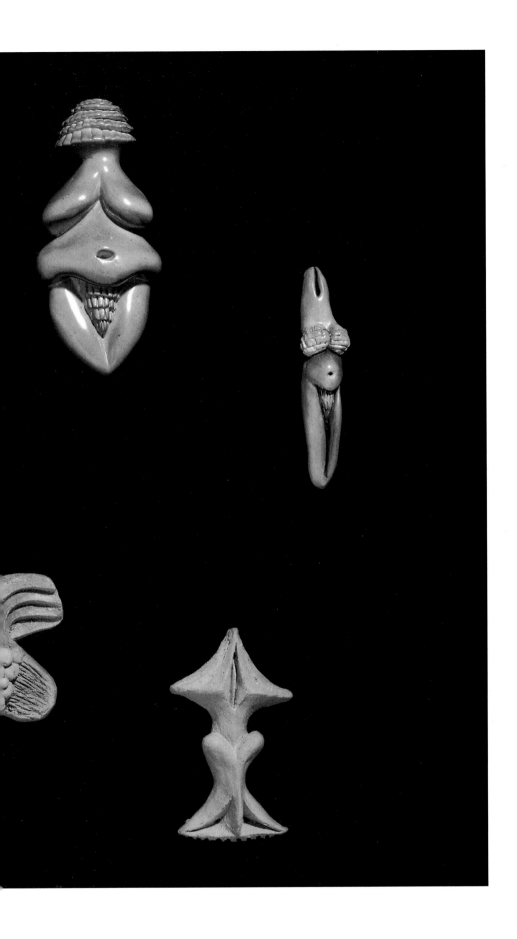

No. 2 - Fertile Goddess - Woman as Fecund and Holy   Judy Chicago 1977

FIG. 131

Judy Chicago. *No. 2—Drawing for Fertile Goddess Plate (Woman as Fecund and Holy),* 1977 (cat. no. 80).

FIG. 132
Rachel Rosenthal. *Gaia Mon Amour*, 1984 (cat. no. 83).

Eating from the *Dinner Party* Plates and Other Myths, Metaphors, and Moments of Lesbian Enunciation in Feminism and Its Art Movement

Laura Cottingham

In heroic days you might have been Joan of
Arc, Madame Roland, Héloïse. But what
might you be today? Try to find a single position in the social hierarchy, on any level of
government or industry, which you might think
of occupying without being ridiculous. Only
the role of artist is open to you.

George Sand, *Letters to Marcie*, 1837

If the thirty-nine women invited to Judy Chicago's *Dinner Party* were to come, some, such as Natalie Barney and Sappho, would arrive as self-identified lesbians; others, such as Emily Dickinson, Virginia Woolf, and Georgia O'Keeffe, would arrive surrounded by a lesbian aura; and others might be silently lesbian. All would participate in a lesbian gesture as they proceeded to eat from the vulvar plates. Just as lesbianism functions as a process involving various psychic, sexual, and social instances of women coming into being (as lesbians), this dinner party metaphor locates lesbian and feminist practices within a shared continuum of coming into being. Lillian Faderman has suggested a continuity between pre-twentieth-century romantic friendships among women and contemporary lesbianism.[1] Borrowing from Faderman and altering her suggestion of continuity, I would like to situate 1970s and contemporary feminist practices within a lesbian continuum. My paradigm assumes that lesbianism occupies neither the deviant biological-psychological category established in academic thought during the nineteenth century nor the exclusively sexual category implied by most contemporary usages. Rather, this paradigm assumes that lesbianism is coextensive with all feminist practice as a nonstatic nomenclature that encompasses women's various efforts toward self-definition and escape from male emotional, economic, sexual, and cultural hegemony.

Feminist Art Program, is, as the quotation marks of its title suggest, a painterly commentary on the cunt rather than a literal representation (it is paired with the similarly abstracted *"Penis"* [1993; fig. 4, cat. no. 21]). Although Chicago and Schapiro were known for their advocacy of cunt-derived forms, the imagery they championed (such as the pre-1970s works of Lee Bontecou, O'Keeffe, and others) and encouraged their students to produce, was always more imagistic and metaphorical than explicit.

It is interesting to consider the reasons for this. Certainly the process that produced Corinne's *Cunt Coloring Book*—the artist drew from life, using friends as models—would have been taboo in the institutional settings that supported Chicago and Schapiro's pedagogy.[22] Apart from societal strictures, a fear that explicit female sexual imagery would be indistinguishable from mainstream pornography also encouraged women to metaphorize

or otherwise aestheticize their images of the female sex. Other works by Corinne, such as her 1982 *Yantras of Womanlove* (see fig. 7, cat. no. 14), a series of solarized photographs of lesbian sexual activities that kaleidoscope into decorative patterns, refrain from the directness that characterizes the coloring book.

A similar dialectic between the explicit and the covert has continued to haunt subsequent women artists who have chosen to work with sexual material. More cerebral than sensual are Millie Wilson's artifacts visualizing aspects of intellectual history and sociology. Unlike 1970s artists such as Corinne, JEB, Betye Lane, and others involved with explicit, usually photographic representations of lesbians, Wilson does not direct her work to an exclusively or primarily lesbian audience. Rather, her lesbianized interactions with surrealism and minimalism are displayed in commercial galleries and act as agents

FIG. 141
Nicole Eisenman. *Amazon Composition*, 1992 (cat. no. 68).

of meaning for a problematized lesbian presence. While Corinne's Yantras of Womanlove idealize lesbian love and sex, Wilson's work documents the sociology of deviance and degradation that circumscribes the historical construction, and contemporary experience, of the lesbian. Her pubic Wigs (1990–92; see fig. 2, cat. no. 16), a series of enormous and elaborate sculptural hairpieces mounted on furniture-finished wooden stands, are based on drawings of clitorises made in 1948 by a male physician who claimed that he could "reveal homosexuality" through the observation of women's genitals. Wilson's cunt-inspired sculptures are more than twice removed from their initial source and are not intended for voyeuristic consumption by either women or men. But then neither are the Meret Oppenheim-inspired fur cunts of Lauren Lesko, such as her Lips series (1993; fig. 10, cat nos. 17–19), or Maureen Connor's delicate organdy wall hanging, *Bishop's Rose* (1980; fig. 9, cat. no. 13).

Like those of many other post-1970s lesbian visual practitioners, Wilson's works are concerned with the quotes around *lesbian*. They are multi-referential, can be visually obtuse, and deliberately refuse to present themselves with the directness

that characterized most of the art made within the feminist art movement of the 1970s. Art produced by women—both lesbians and others—in the United States during the 1980s and early 1990s is more likely to be (visually) ironic. The complications of representing aspects of female sexuality are played out through an aesthetic of irony in works such as Marlene McCarty's 1990 image of the word *cunt* printed, through a process of heat transfer, on canvas (fig. 11, cat. no. 15).

Not all of the younger artists have adopted the distanced strategies favored by Wilson and others. Sue Williams's *A Funny Thing Happened* (1992; fig. 98, cat. no. 69), for example, is as raw, visceral, and biting as anything produced during the 1970s. The work's protective cynicism, however, is at odds with the radical optimism within which so many 1970s works were produced and viewed. Twenty-five years of feminist thinking accompanied by very little political change lend this aggressively feminist painting about rape a certain pathos. Williams presents rape as a perpetual occurrence, not an isolated one, in women's lives. Artists such as Suzanne Lacy and Leslie Labowitz, whose

FIG. 142

Suzanne Lacy and **Leslie Labowitz**. Image from *In Mourning and in Rage*, 1977 (cat. no. 66).

FIG. 143

Scene from *An Oral Herstory of Lesbianism*, 1979, a series of vignettes written and performed by members of the Lesbian Art Project and produced and directed by Terry Wolverton at the Woman's Building, Los Angeles.

Three Weeks in May (1977) and *In Mourning and in Rage* (1977; fig. 142, cat. no. 66) included antirape protests on the steps of the Los Angeles City Hall, assumed that their art and activities could actually help end male sexualized violence against women. Recent history has made such determination and hope seem naive.

Thus, Nicole Eisenman's cartoon-inspired drawings (see fig. 141, cat. no. 68), installations, and murals are less involved with the dreams of a Lesbian Nation that kept lesbians going in the 1970s than they are with Eisenman's own quirky eagerness to have a good time in life and in art—and her suspicion of politics. Such a stance contrasts markedly with the collective political and artistic energies that produced earlier artworks such as *An Oral Herstory of Lesbianism* (1979; see fig. 143), a series of vignettes directed by Terry Wolverton and enacted by thirteen performers before an all-female audience at the Los Angeles Woman's Building as part of the Lesbian Art Project.

It seems clear that none of the feminist-inspired and lesbian artists who emerged during the 1980s and 1990s shares the sense of sisterhood and utopianism that characterize so much of the work of the previous generation. The twenty-five-year gap between the first self-consciously feminist artworks of 1970 and the art of today has produced a gap in sensibilities, if not in political circumstances. So that a work such as Christine Lidrbauch's untitled drawing of 1991 (see fig. 124, cat. no. 30), which invokes what could be called a signature medium of the feminist 1970s—menstrual blood!—has almost nothing but a purely material relationship to precursors such as Chicago's *Menstruation Bathroom* (1972; see fig. 125, cat. no. 24). For, while Chicago's installation rattles the taboos of tampons, sanitary napkins, and monthly cycles, Lidrbauch's drawings are mere decorative constructions.

Nevertheless, some post-1970s artists deliberately reference the work of earlier women practitioners and are conscious of the political ramifications of doing so. For instance, Janine Antoni's

"As women artists

expressing solidarity across differences, we must forge ahead, creating spaces where our work can be seen and evaluated according to standards that reflect our sense of artistic merit. As we strive to enter the mainstream art world, we must feel empowered to vigilantly guard the representation of the woman as artist so that it is never again devalued."

—bell hooks

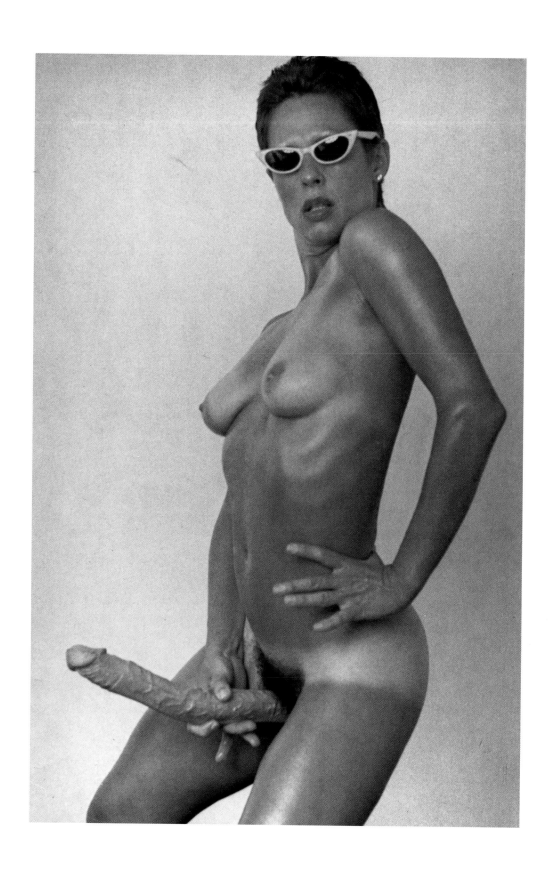

FIG. 147
Lynda Benglis. Advertisement published in *Artforum* (November 1974) (cat. no. 87).

FIG. 148

Faith Ringgold. *#3 The Picnic at Giverny*, from the French Collection I series, 1991 (cat. no. 90).

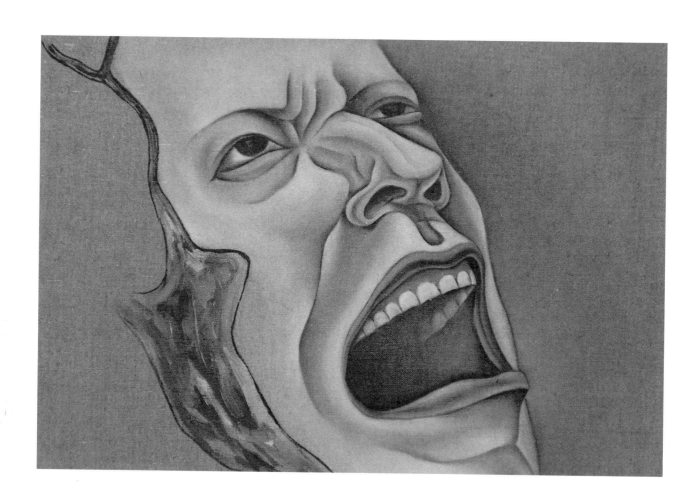

FIG. 149
Judy Chicago. *Disfigured by Power 2*, from the Powerplay series, 1984 (cat. no. 89).

FIG. 150
Karen Finley. *Moral History* (detail), 1994 (cat. no. 92).

FIG. 151
Judith Bernstein. *Five Panel Vertical*, 1973 (cat. no. 86).

FIG. 152
Carole Caroompas. *Spectre and Emanation (Man Hewing His Own Penis from Marble Block)*, 1994 (cat. no. 91).

A Feminist Chronology

1945–95

compiled by
Laura Meyer

1945

The **United States** emerges as the world's leading economic, political, and military power at the close of World War II.

1952

Critic Harold Rosenberg publishes **"The American Action Painters"** in *Art News*, describing the act of painting as a heroic battle for transcendence of the material world.

During the 1950s **abstract expressionism** dominates the New York art world.

1953

The Second Sex, an English translation of Simone de Beauvoir's *Le deuxième sexe*, first published in France in 1949, appears in Great Britain and the United States. The phrase **"women's liberation"** is first used in this book.

1954

The U.S. Supreme Court rules that **race-segregated schools** violate the Fourteenth Amendment.

Oral contraceptives are tested on women volunteers. The research is financed by Katherine Dexter McCormick, who, in 1904, was the second woman to graduate from Massachusetts Institute of Technology.

Twenty million television viewers tune in to the "Army-McCarthy" hearings before a Senate subcommittee investigating charges of subversion made by **Senator Joseph McCarthy** against U.S. army officers and civilian officials.

1955

Rosa Parks refuses to move to the back of a bus in Montgomery, Ala., and is arrested. On the first day of her trial African-Americans begin a boycott of the city's buses.

Adlai Stevenson addresses the Smith College graduating class and urges the women not to define themselves through professional activities, but instead to participate in politics through the **roles of wife and mother.**

1956

Martin Luther King emerges as the leader of the civil rights movement.

Marilyn Monroe is 20th Century Fox's biggest box office draw.

The number of **women in the workforce** has increased from 8.5 million in 1947 to almost 13 million.

Life magazine publishes interviews with five male psychiatrists who argue that **female ambition** is at the root of mental illness in wives, emotional disturbances in husbands, and homosexuality in boys.

1957

The Soviet Union launches *Sputnik*, the first artificial space satellite.

President Eisenhower sends troops to Little Rock, Ark., to keep order during **school desegregation**.

An award-winning series of articles in the *New York Post* documents the existence of an unwritten **ban on contraceptive counseling** in New York City's public hospitals, sustained by the power and influence of the Catholic Church.

Walter Hopps and Edward Kienholz open **Ferus Gallery**, the first professional exhibition space in Los Angeles devoted to local avant-garde art.

1958

· · · · · · · · · ·

Jet airplanes are put into commercial service.

The United States launches its **first earth satellite**, *Explorer I.* NASA is established.

Art News publishes Allan Kaprow's essay "The Legacy of **Jackson Pollock**," paying tribute to the late pioneer of abstract expressionism.

1959

· · · · · · · · · ·

In *The Status Seekers* Vance Packard argues that a **college education** is the wedge dividing white- and blue-collar workers in the United States.

A Century of Higher Education for Women, by Mabel Newcomer, reports that the percentage of **women receiving professional degrees** has not been so low since before World War I.

1960

· · · · · · · · · ·

John F. Kennedy is elected president.

In Ceylon Sirimavo Bandaranaike is elected the **first woman prime minister** of a modern parliamentary government.

Nearly 90 percent of American homes have **television**.

The U.S. Food and Drug Administration gives its approval to the **contraceptive pill.**

The **Student Nonviolent Coordinating Committee** (SNCC) is formed by a group of African-American college students in Raleigh, North Carolina. Sit-ins protesting segregation take place at Woolworth's stores across the country.

Students for a Democratic Society (SDS) is formed in New York.

During the 1960s **pop** and **minimalism** replace abstract expressionism as the dominant artistic styles in the United States. Los Angeles emerges as a major art center.

1961

· · · · · · · · ·

The Soviet Union wins the race to put a **man in space**.

The **Bay of Pigs** invasion of Cuba fails.

At Eleanor Roosevelt's urging, President Kennedy establishes the President's **Commission on the Status of Women**, charged with assessing women's progress and making recommendations for action on employment, social insurance, tax laws, federal and state labor law, and legal treatment.

In his essay "Modernist Painting" Clement Greenberg writes that modern painting must eschew narrative and figurative subject matter, thus establishing the "purity" and "autonomy" of **painting as an optical experience.**

Chouinard Art Institute merges with the Los Angeles Conservatory of Music and becomes the California Institute of the Arts **(CalArts)**.

1962

· · · · · · · · ·

American astronaut **John Glenn** orbits the earth three times in the space-craft *Friendship 7.*

Rachel Carson publishes *Silent Spring*, attacking the careless use of pesticides.

SDS issues a manifesto, drafted by Tom Hayden, calling for participatory democracy to overcome a sense of **powerlessness** in society.

In his essay "Art-as-Art," published in *Art International*, minimalist painter Ad Reinhardt writes, "The one object of fifty years of abstraction is to present **art-as-art** and nothing else . . . making it purer and emptier, more absolute and more exclusive."

Ferus Gallery presents the first solo exhibition of Andy Warhol's **pop art**, showing his Campbell's Soup Can paintings.

1963

· · · · · · · · · ·

Martin Luther King Jr. leads more than 200,000 people on a Freedom March on Washington, D.C., and delivers his **"I have a dream"** speech.

Soviet Cosmonaut Valentina Tereshkhova becomes the **first woman in space**, orbiting the earth forty-five times in the *Vostok 6.*

The Feminine Mystique, by Betty Friedan, becomes a best-seller. Friedan writes that it is time for women "to stop giving lip service to the idea that there are no battles left to be fought for women in America."

In November **President Kennedy is assassinated** in Dallas. Lyndon Johnson becomes president.

Walter Hopps organizes a **Marcel Duchamp** retrospective at the Pasadena Art Museum. The exhibition is memorialized by a photograph showing Duchamp playing chess in the museum gallery with a nude female opponent, Eve Babitz.

1964

Lyndon Johnson is elected president.

In a "Southern strategy" to defeat the Civil Rights Act, Representative Howard W. Smith moves to add **sexual discrimination** to its provisions. After heated debate the House votes to pass the amendment, adding the word *sex* to its bans on discrimination based on race, color, religion, and national origin.

Margaret Chase Smith is the first woman to run for the presidential nomination of a major party. She receives twenty-seven delegate votes at the Republican convention in San Francisco.

Ruby Doris Smith presents a paper entitled "The Position of Women in SNCC" at the organization's staff meeting. SNCC leader Stokely Carmichael responds that **"The only position for women in SNCC is prone."**

1965

African-American activist **Malcolm X is assassinated**.

Thirty people are killed in the **Watts riots** in Los Angeles.

U.S. forces, which have been stationed in **Vietnam** only as military advisers, are authorized for combat for the first time. President Johnson sends 50,000 more troops to Vietnam.

Fifteen thousand **students march** on Washington, protesting the war in Vietnam.

Artforum moves from San Francisco to **Los Angeles** and takes a space upstairs from the Ferus Gallery.

1966

The **National Organization for Women** (NOW) is formed in Washington in response to the government's failure to enforce Title VII of the Civil Rights Act, banning discrimination based on sex. NOW's first president is Betty Friedan.

1967

At the American Medical Association's (AMA) annual meeting, delegates vote to support therapeutic **abortion** under three circumstances: if the pregnancy threatens the physical or mental health of the woman, if the infant might be born with a disabling physical deformity or mental deficiency, or if the pregnancy results from rape or incest. Several states pass liberalized abortion laws following the AMA's new guidelines.

In New York the feminist organization later known as New York Radical Women is formed. The group formulates **"consciousness-raising"** techniques to further the women's movement's goal of empowering women through self-knowledge.

Greenbergian critic Michael Fried criticizes minimalist art in "Art and Objecthood," bemoaning its implicit reference to the **body of the viewer.**

1968

Martin Luther King is assassinated in Memphis.

Robert F. Kennedy is assassinated in Los Angeles.

"Women's liberation" groups begin to form around the country as an outgrowth of the male-dominated student movement. The first independent radical women's newsletter, *Voice of the*

Women's Liberation Movement, is written and published in Chicago. By 1971 there will be more than one hundred **women's movement** journals, newsletters, and newspapers throughout the country.

Josine Ianco Starrels curates the **first West Coast women artists' show**, *25 California Women of Art*, at the Lytton Galleries of Contemporary Art, Los Angeles.

1969

Neil Armstrong and Buzz Aldrin make their historic **walk on the moon**. Says Armstrong, "That's one small step for a man, one giant step for mankind."

U.S. troops in Vietnam number more than 500,000. The massacre of Vietnamese civilians by U.S. Army personnel at My Lai in 1968 is revealed. Some 250,000 **antiwar demonstrators** march on Washington, and another 200,000 gather in Golden Gate Park in San Francisco.

Gay patrons of the Stonewall Inn in New York City fight back when the bar is raided by police. Protest rallies ensue, and many people consider **"Stonewall"** the beginning of the gay and lesbian rights movement.

Canada passes a bill **legalizing abortion and homosexuality.**

The Columbia University Women's Liberation Group releases a report on the **status of female faculty at Columbia**. The study reveals that although one quarter of Columbia's doctoral degrees are awarded to women, only 2 percent of the university's tenured faculty are female.

San Diego State College offers a ten-course program of **women's studies**, believed to be the most comprehensive in the country at the time.

The **FBI** initiates an investigation of the women's movement for possible subversive activity (this fact is revealed in 1977 through an inquiry under the Freedom of Information Act).

In New York, **Women Artists in Revolution** (WAR) forms as a splinter group of the male-dominated Art Workers' Coalition (AWC) when AWC refuses to extend its protests on behalf of minority artists to women.

1970
· · · · · · · · ·

On the fiftieth anniversary of the passage of the Nineteenth Amendment, NOW organizes the **Women's Strike for Equality**. Some 50,000 women march down Fifth Avenue in New York, and more than 100,000 women demonstrate across the country.

The first suit under the Civil Rights Act of 1964 to secure **equal job rights** for women is filed in Toledo, Ohio.

Sisterhood Is Powerful, edited by Robin Morgan; Shulamith Firestone's *A Dialectic of Sex*; and Kate Millett's ***Sexual Politics*** are published.

In New York the Ad Hoc Women Artists' Committee forms to protest the small number of women included in the Whitney Annual and in the Whitney Museum's collections. Thanks to feminist pressure, the **representation of women artists** rises from an average of around 5 percent to 22 percent in the 1971 annual.

Women, Students, and Artists for Black Art Liberation (WSABAL) is founded by Faith Ringgold and her daughter Michele Wallace, helping to launch the **black art movement**.

The Los Angeles Council of Women Artists (LACWA) forms to protest the **exclusion of women artists** from the important *Art and Technology* show at the Los Angeles County Museum of Art. An analysis of the museum's exhibition record reveals that of fifty-three one-artist shows hosted by the museum, only one was dedicated to a woman, photographer Dorothea Lange. On a randomly chosen day, only 1 percent of the art on view at the museum was by women artists.

Judy Chicago establishes the Feminist Art Program at Fresno State College, with fifteen students participating. The curriculum includes feminist consciousness-raising and performance workshops; research into women's history, art, and literature; and radical artistic experimentation.

1971
· · · · · · · ·

Linda Nochlin's ground-breaking essay **"Why Have There Been No Great Women Artists?"** is published in *Art News*. Nochlin argues that patriarchal art institutions have worked to exclude women artists and that women's artwork has been undervalued.

Women in the Arts (WIA) organizes in New York to plan **protests against gallery owners** who do not exhibit work by women artists.

Women in Art Quarterly is founded; after publishing one issue, the staff splits along ideological lines. Some go on to found ***The Feminist Art Journal***.

Where We At: Black Women Artists, billed as the "**first black women's art exhibition**

in known history," is held at Acts of Art Gallery in New York. Organizers include Faith Ringgold, Kay Brown, Jerrolyn Crooks, Pat Davis, Mai Mai Leabua, and Dindga McCannon.

In Washington, D.C., the Corcoran Biennial is devoted exclusively to **work by male artists**. Female artists picket. The Corcoran Gallery agrees to host a conference on women in the arts the following year.

West-East Bag (WEB), an international information-sharing network of women artists, develops out of a visit by Judy Chicago and Miriam Schapiro to Ellen Lanyon, Lucy Lippard, and Marcia Tucker.

June Wayne offers a workshop entitled "Business and Professional Problems of Women Artists" at her Tamarind Avenue Studio in Los Angeles. The workshop develops into a regular series called **"Joan of Art."** Wayne requires that workshop graduates in turn lead seminars for other women artists.

In Fresno the **Feminist Art Program** produces a special issue of *Everywoman* magazine, in which participants describe the program from their own points of view. The program hosts a series of open-house weekends, featuring student performances, art exhibitions, and slide lectures. Program participants also perform at the University of California, Berkeley, and the Richmond Art Center in Oakland.

Judy Chicago and Miriam Schapiro begin a dialogue about **"female imagery,"** visiting artists' studios and documenting the work of women artists.

The new campus of **CalArts** opens in Valencia, fifteen miles north of Los Angeles.

In the fall Chicago and the Fresno students join Schapiro at CalArts, where Chicago and Schapiro lead an expanded **Feminist Art Program**. Rita Yokoi takes over the Feminist Art Program at Fresno. Sheila Levrant de Bretteville, with graduate assistant Suzanne Lacy, founds the Women's Design Program at CalArts.

1972

Richard Nixon is reelected president.

The U.S. Senate passes the **ERA** by a vote of eighty-four to eight and sends the bill to the states for ratification. By the end of the year twenty-two states have ratified the ERA.

Congress passes **Title IX**, which prohibits sex discrimination in educational institutions that receive federal funds.

Representative **Shirley Chisolm** is the first African-American woman to run for the U.S. presidency in a major party primary.

Ms. magazine begins publication.

Stanford University publishes a survey showing that fewer than one out of every twenty-five women graduating from the university in June 1972 expects to be a **full-time homemaker** in 1977. Only 7 percent say they would stop working to raise children. This contrasts markedly with a survey released in 1965, when 70 percent of Stanford women were not planning to work while their children were under six.

At the American Academy of Religion meeting, held in Los Angeles, women theologians call for the "castration of sexist religion." Dr. Mary Daly of Boston College tells a seminar that **patriarchal religion** has led to "a gang rape of our minds."

The women's cooperative **A.I.R. Gallery** is founded in New York.

The **Women's Caucus for Art** (WCA) of the College Art Association (CAA) is founded; Ann Sutherland Harris is the first WCA president.

The Feminist Art Journal, under the direction of editor Cindy Nemser, is founded in New York; the last issue is published in 1978.

In Washington the Corcoran hosts the **Conference on Women in the Arts**.

LACWA negotiates with trustees of the Los Angeles County Museum of Art to hold a historical show of art by women. The proposed exhibition is finally realized in 1976 as *Women Artists: 1550–1950*.

Four Los Angeles Artists, curated by Jane Livingston at the Los Angeles County Museum of Art, gives Maggie Lowe, Barbara Munger, Alexis Smith, and Margaret Wilson their first major public exposure. The exhibition is organized in response to LACWA's demands for **more museum support** of women artists.

The Chicano artists' group ASCO ("nausea" in Spanish)— founded by Patssi Valdez, Willie Herron, Gronk, and Harry Gamboa Jr.— "sign," or vandalize, the Los Angeles County Museum of Art to protest the **exclusion of Latino and Latina artists** from its collections.

Twenty-one Artists: Invisible/Visible, curated by Dextra Frankel and organized by Frankel and Judy Chicago, opens at the Long Beach Museum of Art. Twenty-one **California women artists** are represented.

The CalArts Feminist Art Program hosts the **West Coast Women Artists' Conference**, January 21–23.

Under the direction of Judy Chicago and Miriam Schapiro, Feminist Art Program participants produce **Womanhouse**, a collaborative project in which an abandoned house in Hollywood is transformed into a series of art environments that confront and explore the traditional domestic activities of post-World War II middle-class American women. The project is filmed for public television and written up in *Time* magazine.

1973

The **Watergate** scandal unfolds throughout the year.

Vice-President **Spiro T. Agnew** resigns, pleading guilty to tax evasion.

A U.S. Supreme Court decision in *Roe v. Wade* declares invalid all state laws that restrict abortion in the first three months of pregnancy.

More than three hundred women from twenty-seven countries attend the International Feminist Planning Conference in Cambridge, Mass. The goal of the conference, organized by NOW board member Patricia Burnett, is to build an **international feminist movement** and to organize a full-scale international feminist conference in 1975.

Eight more states **ratify the ERA**, bringing the total to thirty.

In Portland, Ore., 8,600 delegates of the Southern Baptist Church convene for their 116th annual meeting and pass a resolution declaring **male superiority**. It reads in part: "Man was not made for woman, but the woman for the man. Woman is the glory of man. Woman would not have existed without man."

In New York Joyce Kozloff and Nancy Spero publish *The Rip-off File*, a newsletter containing depositions by women in the arts who have

"Saming was the process that was op- erative in that period, looking for how we were the same. When you focus on what is the same, not allowing time to find out how we're different, similarities can become exaggerated. Sexual, ethnic, cultural, eco- nomic, generational differences that separate women from one another were hidden by this focus on the simple fact that we were all biologically women. We thought the cat- egory 'women' could embrace us all."

—Sheila Levrant de Bretteville

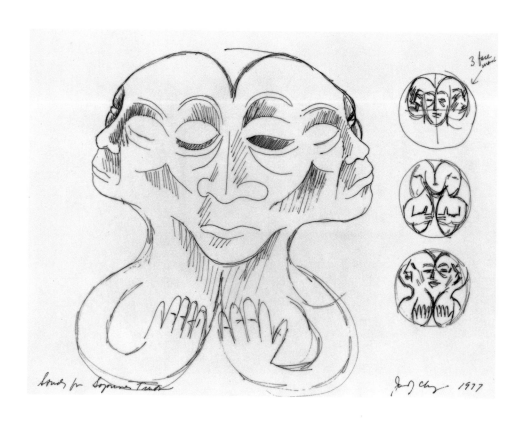

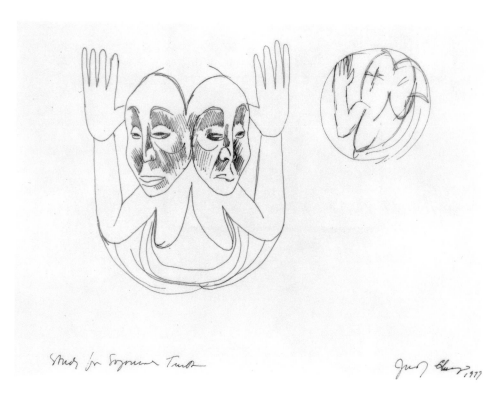

Judy Chicago. *Study for Sojourner Truth #2*, 1977; *Study for Sojourner Truth #4*, 1977 (cat. nos. 95–96).

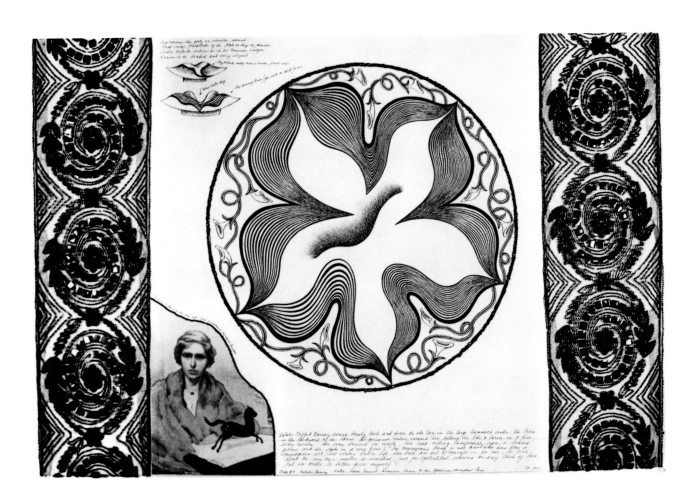

FIG. 155
Judy Chicago. *Study for Natalie Barney Plate and Runner*, c. 1977–78 (cat. no. 97).

FIG. 156

Laura Aguilar. *In Sandy's Room (Self-Portrait)*, 1991 (cat. no. 99).

FIG. 157
Eleanor Antin. *Eleanora Antinova in the Symbolist Ballet "L'esclave,"* from Recollections of My Life with Diaghilev, 1978 (cat. no. 98).

Sources for Quotations

Page 2: Sheila Levrant de Bretteville, interview with Amelia Jones, 22 August 1994; Arlene Raven, interview with Amelia Jones, 13 July 1994; Lucy Lippard, correspondence with Amelia Jones, 20 June 1994; Miriam Schapiro, interview with Amelia Jones, 21 July 1994; Vivian Gornick, quoted in Gwenda Blair, "The Womanly Art of Judy Chicago," *Mademoiselle*, January 1982, 100.

Page 3: Tom Knechtel, interview with Amelia Jones, 28 September 1994; Faith Wilding, interview with Amelia Jones, 13 July 1994; Terry Wolverton, "The Women's Art Movement Today: From the Feminist Art Program to the Woman's Building, Los Angeles Helped Shape the Movement," *Artweek* 21 (8 February 1990): 21; bell hooks, "Women Artists: The Creative Process," in *Art on My Mind: Visual Politics* (New York: New Press, 1995), 131; Arlene Raven, "Women's Art: The Development of a Theoretical Perspective," *Womanspace Journal* 1 (February–March 1973): 14.

Page 13: Faith Wilding, "How the West Was Won," *Images and Issues* 1 (Fall 1980): 15.

Page 39: Judy Chicago, interview with Amelia Jones, 21 June 1994.

Page 75: Miriam Schapiro, interview with Amelia Jones, 21 July 1994.

Page 119: Miriam Schapiro, quoted in Holly Hughes, "Miriam Schapiro: Toward a Feminist Art Education," *Women Artists News* 6 (Summer 1980): 16.

Page 141: Pat Stein, "Anonymous Was a Woman," *LAICA Journal*, no. 1 (June 1974): 34.

Page 177: Mira Schor, "From Liberation to Lack," *Heresies* 24 (1989): 19.

Page 201: Mary Beth Edelson, in "More on Women's Art: An Exchange," *Art in America* 64 (November–December 1976): 13.

Page 229: bell hooks, "Women Artists: The Creative Process," in *Art on My Mind: Visual Politics* (New York: New Press, 1995), 132.

Page 249: Sheila Levrant de Bretteville, interview with Amelia Jones, 22 August 1994.

1996

Despite protests by
students, faculty, and
administrators, the
University of California's
Board of Regents votes
to uphold its July 1995
decision to stop admit-
ting students, hiring
professors, and awarding
contracts on the basis
of race and sex.